Small-scale Outdoor
Pig Breeding

Small-scale Outdoor Pig Breeding

Wendy Scudamore

THE CROWOOD PRESS

First published in 2011 by
The Crowood Press Ltd
Ramsbury, Marlborough
Wiltshire SN8 2HR

www.crowood.com

British Library Cataloguing-in-Publication Data
A catalogue record for this book is available from the British Library.

ISBN 978 1 84797 307 8

Illustrations by Caroline Pratt
Photographs by the author unless indicated otherwise

Frontispiece: Wendy Scudamore with some of her Kunekune pigs
(photo courtesy of George and Dani Clarke, Hi Key Studios)

Typeset by Jean Cussons Typesetting, Diss, Norfolk

Printed and bound in India by Replika Press Pvt Ltd

CONTENTS

DEDICATION

This book is first dedicated to Sybil – my breeding sow, who taught me so much in her short life. Sybil stirred in me the love of pigs which inspires me to get out there, every day, come rain, shine, snow or sickness, and care for my pigs.

Secondly, to all the hundreds of thousands of pigs who languish in indoor pig units across the world – pigs who will never have the joy of nest building, the comfort of a thick straw bed and the delight of earth around their snouts; pigs who will never feel the glory of cold mud on their sun-baked skin.

ACKNOWLEDGEMENTS

My thanks for the support I have received with this book are endless!

First my grateful thanks to Linda MacDonald Brown for her encouragement and enthusiasm, which gave me the incentive to begin writing. Her unstinting support along the way has been invaluable. Thanks also to my family who have learned to cook, clean and generally housekeep while I have sat at my computer! Their love and support is never taken for granted and I hope they will be proud to see the finished product in print.

Many of the photographs have been supplied by others, particularly Liz Shankland, who has helped me so many times – thanks Liz, and to Dani and George Clarke of Hi-Key studios – dear friends and another endless source of support. Thanks to Shirley and Tracey for their hours spent reading and re-reading to give me their valuable feedback.

A special thank you to Dominic Alexander, my vet, not only for his excellent veterinary care but also for allowing me to learn from watching his operations and for supplying me with his own photographs.

And finally, thank you to Marcus Bates of the British Pig Association for permission to reproduce information about the breed standards.

INTRODUCTION

Outdoor pig breeding is a subject rarely covered in depth in available texts.

For many years now I have had the pleasure of taking in other people's sows, mating them with one of my boars and returning them to their owners carrying a litter of piglets. However, when the expected dates of delivery loom closer, my telephone starts to ring, my inbox is unusually full, and the questions begin. I'm happy to help and always tell my customers to treat me as an 'on call' midwife for their pig, but by writing this book, I hope to give all prospective pig breeders the confidence to 'go it alone'. The book has been written to answer all those questions, and the pictures have been included for constant comparison to the reader's own pig, and reassurance that everything is as it should be.

Rest assured that pigs are intelligent, relaxed and sensible creatures, and can and will manage their own reproduction without much help from us – but if you are a small-scale, outdoor pig keeper, then I know it will be important to you to be sure to get everything right, not to cut corners, nor miss opportunities which may compromise the wellbeing of your stock.

Sadly the majority of pigs being bred today are bred in large indoor pig units. Their litters of piglets are produced in very unnatural conditions from conception to weaning, and are subject to an intensive production programme requiring profitable returns and leaving no room for a pig to indulge herself in her natural habits, pastimes and functions.

The sows themselves are short-lived, so everything is geared towards the highest return on the smallest investment. The blame does not lie with the farmers or producers, but with society itself and our demand for 'so much, for so little'.

Take the time to acquaint yourself with pigs, as I have been lucky enough to do: watch their behaviour, hear their constant dialogue, oversee their matings, pregnancies and farrowings, and then allow yourself the luxury of spending time with your litters, getting to know their quirky individualism. When you have done so, I challenge you to walk into a supermarket and come out with a packet of the cheapest sausages, and walk away with a clear conscience. Personally, I don't think it can be done.

If you should decide to breed your pigs, I wish you success, and if I can help any further, please contact me.

CHAPTER 1

FORWARD PLANNING

When I bred from my first Kunekune gilt, Sybil, I asked myself the question: 'If she had ten piglets and I couldn't sell any of them, would I be prepared to keep all ten?' The answer was 'yes'. Had the answer been 'no', then maybe I would never have started breeding pigs. As it was, I was prepared for the possibility that I would be stuck with the whole litter, and I actually only intended having one litter.

Sybil did indeed give birth to ten piglets; nine lived, and all were sold apart from the two we chose to keep. Since then we have never looked back, and after many litters, hundreds of wonderful piglets, many joys and a few tragedies, I will share with you what I have learned so far.

I begin on a cautionary note, as far too often I have seen enthusiastic people start with more than they can cope with, maybe at the wrong time of year, and with little experience under their belts. They bulldoze forwards without giving a lot of thought to what they will do with the piglets, and hoping to glean enough information from friends and neighbours along the way to equip them with the necessary knowledge. This is more a case of crossing the bridges when they manifest themselves, than being prepared for such an

undertaking – and pig breeding is an undertaking. It will involve a financial commitment, a dedication, and a commitment of time and energy.

Anyone who goes into small-scale, outdoor pig breeding thinking they will make a living from breeding and selling piglets will be sorely disappointed. Even the most experienced and successful breeders of pigs don't make a living from piglet sales: there is simply not the demand, the prices are not high enough, and the market is not wide enough to enable you to make sufficient income from the number of pigs that you will be able to produce on a small scale.

Begin your venture with this in mind.

What you *will* be able to do if you do it well and plan carefully is to produce enough piglets to cover all your costs and leave you with a little profit, produce your own sympathetically reared and healthy food, with possibly plenty of it to sell too, and enjoy the pleasures of pig keeping as it should be done.

If you are keen enough to become a breeder of renown, so much the better, but don't put yourself and your pigs under such pressure that the enjoyment and the ethics take a back seat. In other words, 'don't give up the day job'!

WHY AND WHEN TO BREED PIGS

If you intend rearing your pigs for eating, then you should never have the problem of dealing with surplus stock, provided that you don't produce tons of surplus meat. If you are not a meat producer you will need to consider just how many litters you can expect to sell, for what purpose you will sell them, and how you will assess and create a market for them. Time your litters so that you are not dealing with too many piglets for sale at the same time, or too much meat for your outlets.

I have also known many people who have bred from their pigs thinking that they will rear them for the pot, but when the time comes and the piglets are grown they have found it very hard to send them off to slaughter, and in some cases never did. If you intend sending your pigs for slaughter, a word of advice: do not handle or make friends of your piglets. You will remember (if you already have them) how quickly your adult pigs became 'socialized' when they were young, and very young piglets quickly become inquisitive, full of character and highly endearing: it is therefore best to keep a distance from them, and not let them become part of the family!

If you are planning to rear your piglets to sell on as 'pet' pigs or breeding stock, be realistic: pigs for breeding stock need to be good quality animals, and there is a percentage in all litters that will not come up to standard (see Appendix III). These piglets if of a small

Every pig deserves grazing, space, an outdoor life and the correct diet to keep it fit and healthy.

breed will make 'pet pigs' – but think how many piglets you are likely to sell, and what kind of homes you will be wanting for them: there is a healthy market for 'pet pigs', but every pig deserves grazing, space, an outdoor life and the correct diet to keep it fit and healthy. Pigs were never meant to be kept as house pets, and in my opinion should not be kept in this way.

What is the most likely time of year to sell them? Spring and summer are, of course, the seasons when most people look to take on livestock, although during the winter months there are fewer piglets available because summer is the optimum time for breeding. Most people like to breed in the spring, and this is the easiest time to sell, with the whole year ahead of you. It's also the best time to start breeding if you are a novice, as the weather, ground conditions and daylight hours are all in your favour. However, you must think ahead: your piglets will be leaving home ten weeks after they are born (approximately), so if you want to be selling piglets in June, your gilt will need to be farrowing in April, so she will need to visit the boar around Christmas time.

If you are considering showing your animals, then January-born litters will be the better grown for their classes. Consider which, if any, of your sows you may like to show with a litter, and be aware that a sow will always look her best in the show ring if she is pregnant (although not too far on, of course). If you are experienced, it's nice to farrow in the winter as you will then have piglets ready in the early spring when people begin to think of buying.

When starting out I would advise 'staggering' your first litters. Perhaps take one gilt to the boar, then when you collect her, drop off the next, and so on. This will enable you to use your farrowing house and then get it cleared and cleaned in time for your next litter; it will give you ample time to spend with your litter, and it will make sales of your piglets 'flow'. It's better to be a breeder who always has piglets to meet their enquiries than one who has a glut of piglets only once or twice a year. And don't breed so many piglets that you will be prepared to sell them to anyone who comes along, purely so that you are not stuck with them yourself.

When you feel you have come up with answers to all the above questions, prepare yourself well to begin.

WHAT YOU WILL NEED

The financial outlay need not be large: you can start as small as you like and 'grow' as you feel able and when the necessity arises. However, you will need all the basics in place before you commit to buying your stock. The planning of your farrowing house will be covered in a later chapter, but before you even begin, land and buildings are a must. You will need at least an acre of ground to keep and breed pigs on a permanent basis, whatever breed you choose, and outbuildings too. Your pigs may live in an arc or field shelter, but you will need storage space that is dry and clean for your feed, hay, straw and equipment.

Feed and Bedding

Buying feed in bulk bags is a cheaper option, but only advisable if you will be able to use it quickly enough; the vitamins and minerals added to pig food will 'go off' after approximately a month, so be sure that you can use the feed in that time, otherwise buy in smaller quantities. Another economical alternative to buying feed is to buy in 'straights' and mix your own feeds. These can include peas, barley, maize or beans.

Bedding and hay can be stored indefinitely in a dry place, as can other feeds such as stock potatoes or fodder beet.

Pigs love barley straw and will root around in it in winter when there is no grass on the ground. They will eat a fair amount of what you put into their arcs as bedding, but it will keep them occupied and is good for them so be sure to allow them this luxury.

Hay or straw is suitable bedding for pigs, but it must be of a reasonable quality – mouldy, dusty bedding is not good for any animal.

Fencing and Gates

Be sure your fencing is secure and up to the job of keeping pigs in. Some breeds are easier to contain than others, but the very minimum fencing requirement will be good stock fencing, well strained and erected on good strong fence posts. All pigs need their fencing to be close to the ground (so a snout will not fit underneath it!), and a good measure is to put a line of barbed wire along the bottom to prevent the pigs from lifting it with their snouts. In most stock netting the holes are wider at the top than the bottom, so be sure to hang it the correct way up or you may find your piglets wriggling through it!

In winter time when the ground is soft and the pigs are really digging, it is also advisable to run electric fencing round the inside of your fence to stop the pigs from digging too close to it and undermining the fence posts.

Another good precautionary measure with

Good, taut fencing, showing an 'anti-scratching' line of barbed wire.

Two strands of electric tape on a twelve-volt battery. I always use tape as opposed to wire as the pigs can see it more easily.

pig fencing is to run a line of barbed wire around the inside, about 60cm (2ft) up from the ground, to prevent the pigs from using your fence posts as scratching posts.

Alternatively, electric fencing can be used on its own. This is a good way of rotating pigs on your ground, and is tidy and efficient if constructed correctly. For Kunekunes a couple of strands of tape (the type used for keeping horses in) on plastic fence posts is usually sufficient, but for the larger breeds stout fence posts with insulators and at least two, and preferably three strands of fence tape will be necessary. I always use tape as opposed to wire as the pigs can see it more easily. If you choose to use wire, tie some tapes or ribbons at intervals along it until the pigs are clear as to where the boundary fence is.

Set your lower electric fencing line at about the level of the top of the pigs' front legs. They will usually approach it snout first, and once touched, will keep well away from it.

Some pigs will challenge electric fencing to start with, but persevere – if you return them to the pen they will eventually learn to respect

Gate hinge with a pin through the top so the gate cannot be lifted off its hinges.

it. Piglets are the exception, and they will run under the fence, squeal, and repeat the performance again and again!

Ensure your gates are well mounted: on 'L'-shaped gate hinges the pigs may well lift them off with their snouts, and a good tip is to mount the gate with the top 'L' hinge reversed so that it is pointing downwards. This will ensure that the gate cannot be lifted off its hinges. Alternatively, fix a securing pin through the top of one or both hinges.

Metal gates are preferable as they will not rot and cannot be chewed by amorous sows or frustrated boars! If you have larger equipment to move in and out of your paddocks, such as tractors for pulling harrows or for

Gate mounted on a 'lowther' hinge so it cannot be lifted off its hinges.

cleaning out housing, you will need standard-sized 'farm' gates; otherwise pedestrian-sized gates will suffice.

GROUND AND HOUSING

Although pigs are 'grazing' animals, they are quite happy on what you may consider poor quality grazing and will 'browse' and eat a fair amount of what we would class as 'rubbish' – nettles, thistles, and sometimes even docks.

Woodland is an ideal environment for any pig where they can enjoy foraging for all kinds of food. Pigs also love orchards where they can eat the windfalls and live in the shade of the fruit trees in summer. Unlike other livestock, pigs will not do extensive damage to trees. They may rub and scratch, so small trees should be protected with tree guards, but as a rule they will not chew or strip bark from trees. Fence your trees with the same

precautionary measures as you use for your boundary fencing.

The traditional breeds of pig are hardy creatures and will live out all year round, but all pigs are very fond of their home comforts and need a warm, dry arc, shed or barn to sleep in and to shelter from rain in winter and hot sun in summer. There are many different kinds of housing that can be adapted for pigs, although a lot depends on their size and breed: I have heard of people using traditional dog kennels, calf kennels, children's playhouses and stables, to name but a few. However, there are a few guidelines that you will need to bear in mind when choosing or building housing for your pigs:

- Pigs don't like draughts; they like to be cosy in winter
- Galvanized arcs are best sited in the shade to avoid overheating in summer

Traditional-style pig arc with skids for ease of movement, a removable floor for ease of cleaning, and a nice small doorway.

A recycled plastic arc featuring two air vents.

Traditional galvanized arc featuring an offset doorway. Heavy duty, built on an iron frame.

- Adequate ventilation is of the utmost importance to avoid condensation building up inside the housing if there is limited space
- Make sure you buy housing that you can get into yourself – this can be essential for cleaning, attending to a farrowing, or attending a sick pig needing treatment
- Housing that can be moved fairly easily is more convenient
- Sturdy housing is essential. When you buy your piglets they will be small and easily accommodated, but after a few months you will have a somewhat larger animal who will enjoy a good rub or a scratch first thing in the morning – so be sure your housing is up to it!

Pigs are essentially clean animals and will not mess in their beds as long as they have the freedom to go somewhere else, so cleaning a pig house should not be a daily chore; however, bedding will become stale, dusty and compacted, so you will want to refresh it every so often – another reason to make sure that you can get into and out of your pig house with ease. Half an hour bent double in a pig arc full of dust is not fun!

Insulated pig arcs are available and although not absolutely necessary for hardy outdoor pigs, they offer extra comfort in winter and in summer. If you intend farrowing your pigs in an arc, farrowing rails are also an essential item. The rail, which will be positioned fairly close to the base of the arc around the inside, will create a safety 'channel' where the piglets can take refuge if the sow lies down and they are trapped between

Cross-section of an arc to show the positioning and structure of a farrowing rail inside. (Courtesy Bidgiemire Pig Arcs)

This 'pigloo' has a built-in channel for the piglets to escape into when the sow lies down. A detachable crèche on the front provides extra safety for the young litter.

her and the sides of the arc. Some arcs, like the 'Pigloo' photographed, are constructed with a built-in channel for this purpose, in which case a farrowing rail will not be necessary.

If farrowing in an arc, consider attaching a 'crèche' to the door. This will enable the sow to step over and enjoy her freedom at grass whilst keeping the little ones safe, close to the arc. This will be invaluable when the piglets are tiny, as it will give them the freedom to come outside and enjoy the sunshine and rub their little snouts into the dirt, whilst keeping them safe from predators such as buzzards, and from wandering too far away and possibly coming to harm. A crèche can be purchased to fit some housing, but otherwise can be easily constructed from wooden planks or rails.

Floors in pig arcs are optional. If your ground is relatively dry – for example in woodland – and if the arc is well stocked with clean hay or straw, it will be nice and cosy.

An arc with no floor can be easily moved to replace bedding and can be upturned occasionally to air and refresh the inside. However, an arc with a floor will be drier and a lot more economical on bedding, wherever it is sited.

TIME MANAGEMENT AND COMMITMENT

If you are lucky enough to own or rent land adjacent to where you are living, the task of looking after your pigs will be a whole lot easier. If your pigs are part of your full-time occupation then the day-to-day commitment of their feeding and general care will be incorporated into your everyday life. If, however, your pigs are a hobby or 'sideline' in addition to your regular working life, then finding the time, particularly in winter when the days are shorter and the weather is against you, will occasionally be difficult. I know many very dedicated pig keepers who get up long before dawn in the winter months to tend their animals before setting off for work, and are outside tending them again at night, in the dark and the cold, when most people would be sitting in front of a warm fire watching television.

Keeping livestock of any kind is a seven-day-a-week job, and sometimes it can be a night-time job too: pigs will farrow or feel poorly more often than not in the middle of the night or on a bank holiday weekend! So be absolutely sure that you are committed to the demands of a 'farming' lifestyle. Bear in mind also that when you do manage to arrange that well-earned holiday, you will need someone reliable and capable to take care of your pigs while you are away

And finally, if you are going into meat production, think ahead: it won't be long before you are planning the first trip to the abattoir, so find a suitable one in your locality, and make sure you have the correct transport, paperwork and ear tagging ready in advance.

LEGAL REQUIREMENTS

Before you can start to breed your pigs you will have to register with Defra for a herd mark number. This is in addition to the County Parish Holding number that you will already have obtained in order to move pigs on to your property. Every time a pig is moved on or off your premises the official movement document for pigs – the AML2 – must be filled in and copies kept for your records.

It is also a legal requirement to record all medicines given to your animals. Medicine record books are available, although a notebook with dates, drugs and quantities given, and the identity of the animal, will suffice.

You are liable to spot checks from your local Animal Health and Trading Standards office at any time. They will probably want to see all your movement records as well as your medicine record book, and will look at your pigs, possibly checking ear tag numbers.

Ear Tags

Piglets under twelve months of age that are moving off your premises will not legally require ear tagging but can be moved on a temporary mark, such as a coloured stock marker spray. However, any pigs moving to a show ground must be ear tagged regardless of age – even the youngest of piglets must be ear tagged for this purpose.

All pigs over twelve months must be permanently marked by ear tag, tattoo or slap mark to move from one holding to another. Any pigs moving to slaughter must be ear tagged with metal ear tags, not plastic ones. Alternatively, slap markers or tattoos can be used.

Note that for some of the pedigree breeds it

Left: *Button ear tag.* Right: *Metal 'kurl lock' ear tag.*

is compulsory to ear notch piglets that are to be kept as registered breeding stock, and certain breeds do also demand tattoos. All pigs that are pedigree registered must have an ear tag, a tattoo or an ear notch to identify them as a member of their particular herd book. If a pig is not identifiable then it is probably not pedigree, and you should bear this in mind when looking for pedigree breeding stock.

Transport

In order to transport your pigs you will need a suitable trailer. It need not be an expensive livestock trailer but it will need to be of sturdy construction with a roof, ventilation, sound floor and sides, and a ramp and holding gates. This must be a trailer which can be disinfected between journeys as it is a legal requirement to thoroughly clean and disinfect it before and after every journey. It is not legal to transport pigs in the back of a car as this cannot be disinfected. If travelling piglets in a car they must be in a container that can be disinfected.

THINK AHEAD

Should you decide to start breeding your pigs, think ahead, plan carefully, and start small, is the best advice I can offer. If after a couple of years you feel that things are working out really well and you are finding pig breeding enjoyable and worthwhile, it will be easy to expand your breeding stock and let your venture grow.

Get to know your pigs well so that you know what to expect from them – those that have had a problem may well have the same problems next time around. Being well organized and well prepared may prevent the problems from reoccurring. Keep careful records – breeding record books are cheap and will remind you of all the important things you need to record.

After reading this book I hope you will be able to plan your timetable, land, farrowing quarters, show seasons and potential litters, and keep careful records of your sows' seasons, matings, farrowings and any complications that may arise.

CHAPTER 2

CHOOSING YOUR BREEDING STOCK

Choosing a breed of pig can be difficult – they are all so nice! However, your choice can be narrowed down by finding a breed that is well suited to your purpose, environment, experience (as some breeds are easier to handle than others) and, of course, your preference.

There are many breeds of pig and we all have our personal favourites, be it the traditional Gloucester Old Spot with her wonderful bustling shape and huge ears and docile nature, or the mischievous Tamworth with her prick ears, inquisitive eye and constant search for entertainment! (*See* Appendix III 'Breeds of Pig' for detailed information of each breed.) With such a wide and varied choice it is important to research the breeds carefully and find out which will suit you the best. There are pigs that will clear land more efficiently than others, some that are hardier than others, and others that are more inclined to graze. Temperaments vary, as do mothering skills and adaptability.

A good plan is to go to some agricultural shows and meet the different breeds personally – the pig lines at an agricultural show are one of the most popular areas of the entire show. They are only closed to the public during the showing classes when the pigs are being guided in and out of the building: at all other times you are invited to walk through and admire the breeds. Most breed societies will have a small stand in the building to display information and pictures about their breed. You may find leaflets to give you more information, and of course there will always be breeders on hand to answer your questions.

Once you have settled on a breed, choose a breeder with a good reputation who will freely offer follow-up help and advice. This will be invaluable in the long run.

Choose your breeding stock with care – we will look into selecting your boar later on, but pick your gilts carefully: don't be attracted to the tiny runt of the litter if you are hoping to go into breeding – rather, go for well-made, well-grown, healthy, bright piglets. Look at the important traits that you would want your gilt to pass on to her offspring: good feet, a well-aligned jaw, good eyesight and hearing, and, most importantly, a good breeding 'underline'.

It is best to breed only from gilts that have at least twelve evenly spaced teats, and some breed societies will demand that gilts have fourteen teats in order to be pedigree registered for breeding (*see* Appendix III). Some breeds have large litters and each piglet will need its own teat to feed from; furthermore not all teats on every sow will

A typical breed society show stand in the pig lines covering information on the breed.

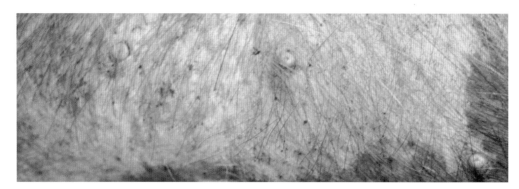

The two left-hand teats are 'blind' and have a flat appearance compared with the good teat on the right.

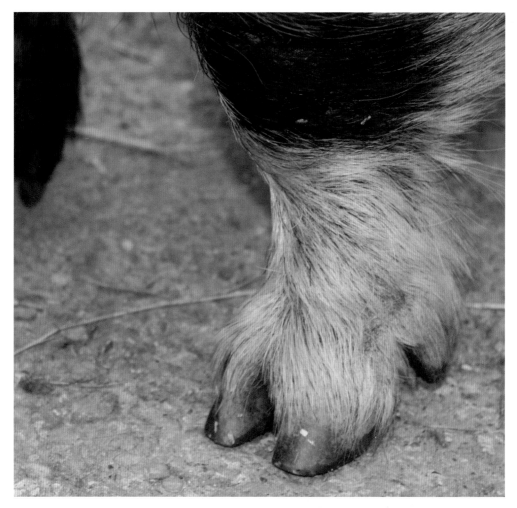

This boar has good, upright feet; there is no overgrowth of the foot, and he stands well up on his pasterns.

function, so it is useful to have a few 'spares' to fall back on!

The little Kunekune pig generally has smaller litters, and the breed standard does state 'at least ten' evenly spaced teats. But there are exceptions to every rule, and I have heard of Kunes giving birth to as many as seventeen piglets in a litter. Teats are important when choosing a boar, too, because he will pass this gene on to his gilt piglets.

Always buy pedigree, registered stock: the price will be a little higher but your offspring will be worth more as a result, and of course no offspring should be sold on as breeding stock if they are not registered pedigree.

Buying pedigree stock is a guarantee that you know what you are getting. Buying from a breeder who is conscientious enough to register their stock should give you more confidence in the long-term aftercare you can expect from them.

When you come to choose a boar for mating with your sows, bear in mind that many owners of pedigree boars, myself included, will not allow their boar to cover unregistered pigs, even if they appear to be of the same breed.

There are many people who will argue that registration is unnecessary, particularly if breeding for meat, but look at it this way: registration is cheap, easy to do, and protects the breeds that we love. Many a gilt and boar has been sold on for 'finishing' only to be kept on and bred from at a later date.

By registering and breeding to a tight registration programme you will not only protect those breeds, you will also open up more possibilities of what you can do with your progeny should you wish to show or export them, or just sell them on to other breeders for breeding.

SELECTING AND KEEPING YOUR OWN BOAR

Artificial insemination (AI) is a common way of breeding pigs on a large scale, although this is not yet available for all breeds. At the time of writing, AI is available for the Berkshire, British Saddleback, Large Black, Middle White, Tamworth and Gloucester Old Spot (*see also* Appendix III).

Most small scale pig keepers will either keep their own boar or will source a good boar at stud. Sourcing a suitable pedigree boar is not difficult through the relevant breed society. For different pedigree breeds there is usually a 'boars at stud' list available on the British Pig Association website, which links to each breed society. For the Kunekune a list can be found on the society website (*see* Useful Addresses) and in the quarterly newsletter.

You will need to be a member of your breed society or the British Pig Association in order to register your piglets as pedigree.

There are advantages and disadvantages to keeping your own boar. The main advantage is the ease and convenience of having a boar on site, ready to mate at any time of year with any or all of your sows. It is also good to get to know your boar, to spend time with him so you are sure of his temperament, and to keep him in good health.

Another advantage of having your own boar is keeping a 'closed herd', rather than bringing in a boar from outside, which can, of course, bring in disease, or having to send your sow away to stud where she may come into contact with disease. Sending your sow or sows away may also present problems with leaving other stock at home, which will in turn have to be reintroduced to one another on the sow's return. This can sometimes be difficult, as fighting can occur. For the small-scale pig keeper there is also the issue of transport and transporters regulations (*see* Useful Addresses for the Welfare of Animals in Transit – WIT – guidelines).

At the time of writing there is a twenty-one-day 'standstill' on pigs, so by having your own boar on site you will avoid the problems associated with pig movements on and off your premises.

There are, however, disadvantages to keeping your own boar, the main drawback being that you will be constantly reproducing the same genes. Thus if you have mated your sow to your boar and would like to keep back some young gilts from your litter for next year's breeding, these will not be compatible with your boar unless you are willing to 'line breed'; we will look into this issue later in this chapter. Using other stud boars or AI gives you a far greater selection of genes and bloodlines to choose from, and also enables you to keep back your own female stock for breeding.

Having your own boar can be costly, and you will need to take into account the cost of his feed, wormers, vaccinations, bedding, and any vets' bills he may incur. Even without vets' bills, the cost of feed, bedding and routine wormer for a boar for twelve months is several hundred pounds at the time of writing.

He will also need company: a castrate, a barren sow or an in-pig sow can live with a boar, although to keep changing his companion can create problems of fighting, as mature boars can become territorial and dominant. If keeping a castrate specifically as company for your boar you will also need to take his keep into account when calculating the costs of keeping a boar.

Another problem is that very occasionally a boar will worry his companion and mount him. If the companion pig reciprocates and stands for the boar this can cause problems, at worst leading to a rectal prolapse in the castrate. If the boar persists in this type of behaviour, you will have to separate him and keep him alone where he can see other pigs but not interact with them.

You will also need excellent fencing in order to keep your gilts and sows separate from your boar.

Handling a Boar

Some boars of the larger breeds can be difficult to handle and are perhaps not suitable for novice pig keepers. All boars should be treated with great respect: no matter how docile a boar may be, always remember he is

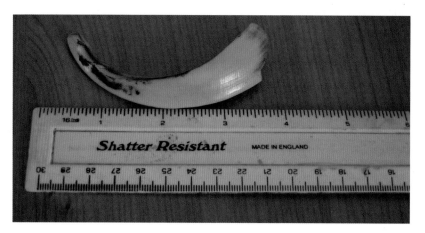

Tusk taken from a mature boar. Tusks are thick and sharp and capable of doing serious damage.

Whether at home or at a show, a boar should always be handled by two adults equipped with boards and sticks. (Courtesy Quantock Kunekunes)

a walking mass of testosterone and his behaviour may be unpredictable. Ideally, when handling a boar, two adults should be present and pig boards available.

All boars, castrated or entire, will grow tusks which protrude from the sides of the mouth and can cause extensive damage when fighting. These can be removed by an experienced vet with very little trouble. The tusk is sawn off at the base, very close to the gum, whilst the pig is restrained with a snare (rope) around his upper jaw. There is no need to anaesthetize the boar for this procedure as long as vet and handler are experienced.

In Summary

- The advantages of having your own boar are that you can keep a closed herd, it is more convenient and possibly cheaper, and you can handle and get to know the boar
- The disadvantages are that you will be reproducing the same genes, which will lead to incompatibility with your own stock; there is the inconvenience of keeping pigs separated; and there are the extra costs involved, including possible vets' bills

HOW CLOSE TO BREED

So we must choose which boar to use, but before we discuss conformation and temperament, we need to look at relationships.

There are many different views on how closely related a boar and sow should be. It is fair to say that if you are breeding 'close' you will multiply the bad genes as well as the good. I prefer to 'outcross' – bring in unrelated boars – and accept the bad with the good; outcrossing can be used to gain a special feature from another strain, or to correct a recurring fault, either in the physical make-up or temperament. This can produce very mixed results, including offspring that are most disappointing, or some outstanding progeny.

Alternatively you can linebreed, which is breeding back through the generations to a known good animal. For example, if the boar you began your breeding with is the great grandfather of your gilt, she may be mated back to him in order to multiply his good genes in her breeding line. This is a more controlled method of breeding, which does produce good results as long as you are sure of the quality of the chosen stud to which you are linebreeding. If you mate a good animal with an equally good animal you can expect to produce some good offspring.

Linebreeding is a good method of testing the suitability of your boar for his job; if he is bred closely to his mother, for example, you may 'bring out' any genetic problems. Mating relatives will concentrate their genes, whether good or bad.

Inbreeding is the mating of close relatives without introducing any fresh blood: father to daughter, mother to son, brother to sister, and the resulting progeny are always larger than the original stock and have increased vigour. However, inbreeding tends to produce rather highly strung animals and they often do not 'do' well.

If inbreeding levels are kept low there will

Piglet with a partly formed snout with only one nostril; it is also missing an eye on the left side of its head.

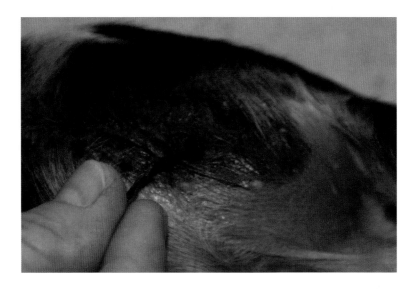

Although this piglet appears to be male from the back end, he was born with neither penis nor anus.

be few problems. However, once inbreeding builds up, genetic defects may appear, and if you keep on inbreeding you will see 'inbreeding depression', where fertility and survival deteriorate.

Inbreeding is a technique used to multiply the positive or 'good' genes. Unfortunately it does the same with the bad genes and can produce congenital abnormalities such as cleft palate, blind anus, hernia, and heart, eye and ear problems, and obvious physical deformities too. Therefore breeding this closely also involves a serious need to 'cull' the piglets that display these 'imperfections'.

This is a thought-provoking subject with many advantages and disadvantages. It is certainly best left to those with an extensive knowledge of pedigrees and genetics, and those who are willing to cull their imperfect stock.

Personally I don't like close breeding, so with my own choice of breed, the Kunekune, which has a gene pool that is already limited (bearing in mind that all the Kunekunes in Great Britain today are descended from fewer than twenty pigs imported in the early 1990s), I would advise that when selecting a boar you find one that is not closely related to your gilt. The simple way to do this is to compare the pedigrees. You will not want to mate your sow with a boar that is the same male bloodline as your sow's father, and you need also to look at the bloodline of the boar's mother. Do not choose a boar whose mother is the same line as your sow.

Many of the traditional breeds are also of limited gene pools, so as a safety measure I would apply the same rule to all. Some have different systems of monitoring the bloodlines and breeding in order to avoid the problems of inbreeding.

GENERAL APPEARANCE AND CHARACTERISTICS

If there are any characteristics which you don't like about your pig or which are perhaps bad traits of the breed, then try to find a boar that complements them. For example, if you have a Kunekune gilt with a rather long nose you would do well to put her to a boar with a nice, short, slightly squashed face; if she is a little long in the leg, then try to find a short dumpy chap.

Choose a boar with good feet, as he will pass these on to his offspring, and be sure to check his underline – a boar needs to have good, well spaced teats. If he has bad teating, his daughters (as well as his sons) may inherit this defect.

Always be sure of the boar's temperament. Ideally he should be docile and friendly. With the Kunekune, temperament is mentioned on the breed standard and is therefore an important trait of the breed and one which should be bred in rather than out. Any boar of any breed which is known to be aggressive should also be avoided: aggression is a trait that may be passed on and should always be bred out.

Overall, use the best quality boar you can find, and if you are buying a boar it is particularly important to choose a good specimen. Remember that your boar is half your herd, so it is important that he is as good, if not better quality than your sows. It is advisable to refer to the breed 'standard of perfection' when choosing a boar. We rely on the breeder of the boar to have selected him specifically because he is a good specimen of the breed.

If you choose to use a boar which is not registered, he will not necessarily have arrived in his job by virtue of his being a beautiful specimen of the breed! There are

---

In Summary

- **Outcrossing** is the mating of unrelated animals: it is a procedure normally used to gain a special feature from another strain, or to correct a recurring fault, either in the physical make-up or temperament. This can sometimes result in offspring that are most disappointing, or it can produce some outstanding progeny
- **Inbreeding** is the mating of close relatives without introducing any fresh blood, father to daughter, mother to son, brother to sister. It can produce deformities and abnormalities, and eventually may lead to inbreeding depression
- **Linebreeding** is breeding in lines that lead back over three or four generations to a known good animal. This is a better method than inbreeding as long as you are sure of the quality of the chosen stud to which you are linebreeding

Dr Rex Walters is the genetics consultant to the British Pig Association. At a recent convention he said the following of breeding pigs: 'Crossbreeding is a better alternative to inbreeding, even for backyard pig farms.' He also said that while inbreeding – allowing boar and sow from the same breeding to mate and reproduce – is commonly practised by pig farms, it increases the possibilities of animal defects and a lesser litter yield per year. Crossbreeding, however, improves the survival rate of piglets and increases by about 6 per cent the litter size per year.

Walters maintained that the use of good genetics for production would result in a large number of pigs per year, as well as fast and efficient growth. He also said that good genetics would result in pigs with big appetites, which in turn would lead to better quality pork. (International Conference of Pig Breeding, Ukraine, 2007.)

Champion boar Barton Hill Tutaki IX, belonging to the author. Always choose the best quality boar you can find.

many boars who have found their way into their occupation purely by accident.

Look at as many boars as you feel you need to, and choose carefully.

Boars should be kept in a healthy condition, especially if they are being used for stud purposes; regular worming and de-lousing should be a matter of course. De-tusking is also sometimes necessary to prevent damage to the sow, and the boar's weight should be kept under control as an overweight boar can seriously damage a sow's back or pelvis.

If sending your gilts to stud, be sure to ask for the dates of matings and the expected dates of farrowing, as this will be really important to you when the time comes. There is nothing worse than playing a 'waiting game' for weeks on end and then finding that your gilt was not expecting a litter at all!

CHAPTER 3

HOGGING AND MATING

The mating of pigs is a topic not often covered in modern literature due to the wide use of artificial insemination. In this chapter we will look at the different options available to you when deciding to mate your pigs. However you decide to go about the mating process, you will need to be familiar with the breeding cycle of the female pig, the physical nature of the gilt that is ready to breed, and the care of pigs during mating.

A sow that breeds regularly (two litters a year) will stay in optimum breeding condition. She will be at her most fertile in the first season following the weaning of her litter (at approximately eight weeks of age) and this is the ideal time to return her to the boar. If she is particularly poor, having fed a large litter, the first season can be missed, although it is unwise to leave older sows any longer than this as they will soon build up internal fat around the ovaries and will cease ovulating and therefore not conceive again. There will be time for her to gain condition again when she is in pig.

If you are thinking seriously about going into breeding it is worth considering the option of buying a sow that is in pig, as you are then at least guaranteed that she is not barren and you will spare yourself the long wait while a young gilt matures to breeding age.

The optimum age to start breeding from a gilt is twelve to eighteen months – any younger than twelve months and the gilt is really not mature enough to have a litter.

HOGGING

A 'gilt' is a female pig that has never had a litter of piglets; a 'sow' is a female pig that has had piglets. For ease of writing I will refer in this chapter to the female pig as a 'gilt'.

'Hogging' is the term used for a female pig that is ready to mate, or 'in season'. Whether taking in a boar for stud purposes, using artificial insemination, or sending your gilt away for mating, it is essential to be able to recognize when your gilt is in season or 'hogging'.

If you are intending to send her away to stud it is helpful to recognize when she is hogging as you can then arrange to deliver her to the boar at the correct time in her cycle; if you take her to the boar when she is already hogging, she will be unlikely to conceive at this time as travelling can often upset the gilt. This will mean a much extended stay for her at the boar's premises as it will be a further twenty-one days before she can be put to the boar again.

A journey in the trailer will often bring a gilt into season, so if you transport her to the boar

Smaller breeds can become sexually mature earlier so it is important to separate entire male piglets from female piglets at weaning.

approximately one week before her heat is due, she will probably come hogging within a few days of her arrival.

Hogging occurs every twenty days all year round from the age of about six months, although it can begin at any time after about three months of age; therefore gilts left in a litter with uncastrated males can become pregnant. The age when a pig becomes sexually active varies from about three or four months of age up to sixteen to eighteen months, although it is usual for a gilt to show her first signs of hogging between six and twelve months. Different breeds of pig differ in this respect.

A young boar's testicles can descend at any time from about three months of age to eighteen months. Some boars will retain one or both testicles, but they may still possibly be fertile. However, you would never intentionally breed from a boar with this problem as it is an undesirable trait that he may pass on to his sons.

Some gilts will have an irregular cycle, and some may not come hogging at all.

The heat will last approximately forty-eight hours from start to finish, although signs of hogging may be obvious for several days either side of the fertile period, during which the gilt will stand for mating and will conceive a litter. The optimum time to mate is actually the second day of the 'true heat', as ovulation takes place about thirty-six hours into the heat.

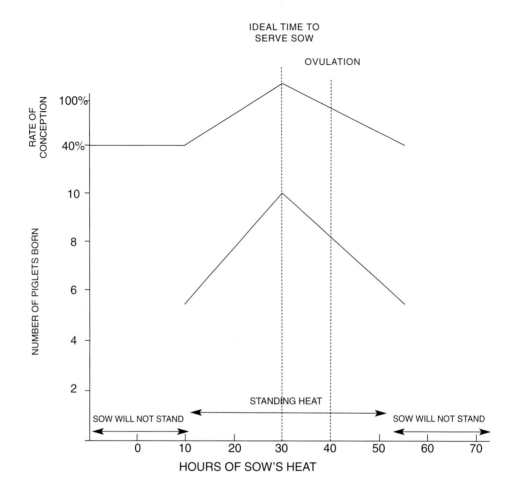

Chart showing the ideal time to serve your sow.

What we call 'standing heat' is when the gilt will stand for the boar to mount her. This can be detected by applying pressure to the back of the gilt, just behind the hip joint; if she is ready to be served she will stand absolutely still and will allow you to put considerable pressure on her back.

Signs of hogging may not be obvious in a maiden gilt, particularly if she is not near to a boar, though she may 'show' more if she is in close proximity to other sows that are cycling regularly. Look out for the following signs:

■ Swelling of the vulva and clear discharge from the vulva
■ Unruly behaviour, especially noisiness
■ A tendency to stand very still and twitch the tail

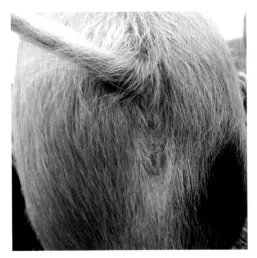

This gilt is not in season.

The same gilt when 'hogging' or in season. Note the swelling and reddening of the vulva.

- A vocal sound not unlike 'barking' if you push at the gilt gently with your knee in the side of her tummy
- A refusal to move when excessive pressure is applied to her back

Your pig may show some, or none, or all of these signs, but if you don't notice any of them don't assume that she has never come hogging. When a gilt is in close proximity to a boar her hogging will be much more recognizable, particularly the changes in behaviour.

Very occasionally a gilt will not come hogging at all. If this is the case you can ask for hormone treatment from your vet, which should produce a 'season' within a few days. This does not, however, guarantee that she will be fertile.

ARTIFICIAL INSEMINATION (AI)

AI is suitable, cheap and convenient for large-scale pig breeders, and some small-scale outdoor pig breeders also choose to use it.

Courses on AI are now available, as are instruction manuals and videos. However, for the novice pig keeper on a small scale AI may have its problems, the first of which is that first-time gilts will not always be receptive and therefore not so easy to inseminate.

Artificial insemination requires a skilled pig keeper who can recognize exactly when his pig is receptive and fertile. Sperm must be kept at the optimum temperature, and used within a certain timescale. If you are not practised in AI you may inadvertently waste a lot of sperm before you are successful in your attempts to impregnate your pig; thus for the inexperienced pig keeper it may well be cheaper and easier to hire a boar's services than to waste sperm on failed attempts at AI.

If you choose to use the artificial method you will need to recognize when your gilt is hogging so that you can order the semen from the supplier in time for her next cycle. Semen will be sent to you in a package with instructions for use, catheters, and enough semen for several attempts at serving. Before attempting to inseminate your gilt you will need to observe her behaviour and detect when she is ready to accept mating by testing her for 'standing' heat.

As with all methods of mating, record the insemination date and observe your gilt twenty days later to see if she comes hogging again.

INTRODUCING BOAR AND SOW

If you should decide to go the natural route with your mating, you will have to decide if you are willing to have the boar at home, or if you would prefer to take your sow to stud; and once you have sourced a suitable boar, you will need to find out if the owner prefers to take sows in to stud, or to loan the boar out.

If you should decide to borrow a boar and bring him home, be sure to be organized. It is not a good idea, particularly if you are a beginner, just to leave the pigs to 'run' together: many people start out this way, assuming that the pigs will bond and mate, and that all will go according to plan – and four months later find themselves wondering what went wrong! It is therefore important, particularly with your first litter, to know when the deed is done so that you can work out the due date and know exactly when to expect your piglets.

Apart from the obvious problem of not knowing when your gilt is due to farrow, there is also the possibility of initial fighting. Furthermore, most boars will show keen interest when put into a paddock with a gilt or sow, regardless of whether she is hogging, and she may be chased round the paddock for hours on end: if she is not yet willing to stand, injuries to legs, hips and back can occur.

Never introduce pigs in a small, confined space unless you are absolutely sure of the following:

- The sow is ready to stand for the boar
- The sow is not aggressive in any way
- The boar is experienced and not aggressive
- There is no trace of the scent of another boar in the pen

Initially, I would advise putting the boar into a neighbouring paddock to the gilt, where they can see and smell one another. When the time is right to introduce them, take the gilt into the boar's paddock or quarters, and not the other way round, as the boar may waste a lot of time marking the territory and scenting, instead of getting on with the job of mating. In his own paddock or quarters he will have no need to do this as he will already 'own' the territory.

Occasionally a gilt will seem quite frightened of the boar until she shows signs of 'hogging'. Again, if at all possible keep the two in neighbouring paddocks. However, if this is not possible, I would emphasize again, introduce them carefully and slowly so as not to frighten her. If the gilt seems unusually frightened, stressed or agitated, remove her from the boar's paddock and try again later.

Sows (females that have bred before) can sometimes be aggressive towards the boar if they are not receptive to him, and I have seen a sow attack a boar quite viciously on more than one occasion. This behaviour is only temporary and as soon as the sow is hogging she will accept a boar without question or anxiety, and all fear and aggression will quickly become a distant memory! It is, however, worth being cautious and leaving introductions until the sow is hogging, because if fighting occurs, either pig may get injured.

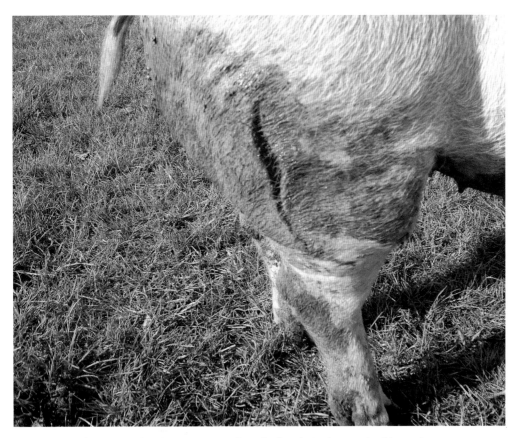

An example of the extensive damage one swipe of a boar's tusks can do. Always be cautious when introducing boar to sow. (Courtesy Tracey Jaine, Northmoor Rare Breeds)

For the benefit of those who are thinking of keeping a boar of their own, or even just bringing a boar in, at this point I have to say that I have far more trouble keeping hogging gilts out of the boar's paddock than I do keeping the boar out of the gilts' paddocks. It seems that when a pig is hogging she has an overwhelming instinct to get to a boar and breed. I have seen sows chew on wire fencing to try to get through to a boar, chew gates to the point of ruin, and I have on one occasion had a sow of my own scale a four foot wall, scramble down and land in a pond the other side. Fortunately the pond was fairly shallow and she was none the worse for it. She was, however, pregnant!

My advice is to keep the sows well away from the boar unless you are trying to bring them into season – I like to keep at least two paddocks between sow and boar so if there is a mishap I will find out about it before any pig makes it through the second fence!

Another word of warning: if a mature boar is interested in a sow and is making up to her through a fence, beware that his tusks don't get caught in the wire – I find this happens with alarming regularity to boars with long tusks, and it is a distressing situation to deal with whilst the boar is screaming and his mouth is bleeding! A pair of efficient wire cutters will soon put it to rights, but the poor boar may suffer nasty injuries to his teeth and mouth. A strand of electric wire is a good deterrent for this, and may save you having to cut holes in your precious fencing.

MARKING TERRITORY AND SCENTING

The instinct to mark territory with scent glands is an important part of a boar's mating ritual, and he will go through this performance whenever he is introduced to new territory, particularly if he can see or smell the presence of another boar.

Boars have scent glands in the mouth and on the forelegs; when scenting with his mouth, a boar can give the impression that he is biting or being aggressive – he is not, but he will take hold of anything he can find, particularly on the perimeter of his territory, and coat it in his saliva. He will work his jaw continuously and will slobber white foam that smells quite strong, although not particularly unpleasant.

My boars will often walk their fence line and hold the wire, gate, scratching posts or trees and bushes in their mouths to 'mark' their territory. They also have a habit of grabbing my boots when I am close by, which can be rather startling if you are not expecting it.

The boar will also trickle urine almost continuously whilst marking his territory, and this has an extremely strong and very unpleasant odour.

There is another form of scenting that I refer to as 'getting ready for the charge'! On the inside of the forelegs you will find several little holes: these are scent glands, and a boar can often be seen rubbing his front trotters back and forth along the ground with his shoulders hunched, the hair along the back of his neck standing straight up, and his head

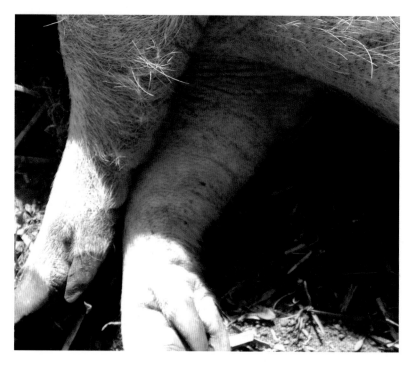

The small holes that can be seen on the inside of the boar's front legs are scent glands.

down so he looks as if he is preparing himself to charge. He is actually not going to charge, but is secreting scent from these little glands in his legs on to the ground, again to 'mark' his territory.

The secretion from these glands is a strong smell to a boar or sow, and even if you yourself cannot smell it, the pigs can; beware of using tools or handling equipment with a boar if you have not cleaned them since handling another boar previously. If you make this mistake, your boar may attack the equipment simply because he can smell what he thinks is the presence of another pig. Apart from making him difficult for you to handle, this may also make him behave in an aggressive manner, simply because he believes another boar is in close proximity.

When moving your boar from one place to another, always use the correct equipment – a board and stick.

When the territorial ritual is complete, the boar will be ready for mating.

FLUSHING

'Flushing' is a term that describes giving extra feed rations to the gilt just prior to mating. By feeding extra protein (up to double the normal ration) for about two weeks prior to mating, you will ensure that your pig is in good condition. This effectively will tell her body that she can afford to develop many embryos and she will therefore have the best chance you can give her of conceiving a good litter.

Worming prior to flushing is extremely important: no amount of food and care will keep your sows in good condition if they are carrying a worm burden, and your sows should not be sent off to stud without first worming them. This worming, prior to mating, will see the sow through to farrowing time.

Cease the flushing as soon as the mating is completed, but ensure that the sow is still on a good diet, as she will now need to develop a good, healthy placenta to feed all those developing piglets.

This is a tried and tested method which ensures the best possible conception rate, and is used in other livestock, too.

MATING

Pigs will ovulate on the second day of their heat – that is, the second day on which they will stand for the boar. Sperm from the boar will develop and fertilize the eggs about six hours after ejaculation, so the optimum time to mate your sow will be the morning of the second day of her heat (*see* chart earlier in this chapter).

There will be a period of courtship with most matings when the boar will scent the gilt, become excited, and mount and dismount from her several times. Don't interrupt his courtship, but allow him to continue with what for him and his gilt is an entirely natural practice – and under no circumstances interfere with the mating, although I would advise that you do observe the mating to be sure that it has taken place successfully.

There are two ejaculations during a mating: the first is an amber-coloured fluid which flushes through the boar, clearing urine and bacterial residue which is harmful to semen; consequently this fluid is high in bacteria. It can be a considerable amount – up to 100ml in an older boar. In a young boar there may only be about 10–20ml of this fluid, which comes from the preputial sac. Once this ejaculation has taken place the boar will begin to thrust, and his corkscrew-like penis will lock into the coil-like cervix of the gilt. A thick gel from the seminal vesicles will form a seal between the ridges of the boar's penis and the coils of the cervix; this gel will prevent any

It is advisable to watch mating take place. This boar is 'resting' following mating, until he is able to disengage from the sow and dismount.

contamination of the sperm by the fluid from the preputial sac. The ejaculation of sperm will quickly follow.

The boar will then 'rest' in this position for some time, until his erection subsides and he is 'released' from the cervix of the gilt.

The mating can take up to about twenty minutes.

If your boar appears to be having difficulty in entering the gilt, particularly if he is young and inexperienced, it is possible to guide his penis into the gilt's vagina to be sure that he has made entry and the penis locks into the cervix. Very occasionally the boar's penis will enter the anus, and this should be avoided.

Once the mating has taken place I usually take the gilt away from the boar and return her to him again later in the day. The purpose of this is to keep the boar 'fresh', as some gilts can persistently worry the boar even after he has mated with them, which can at best give the boar no peace and at worst lead to fighting. A boar will need several hours to rest between matings, and if returned to the gilt half a day later, he will be ready to serve her again.

If this is not possible, then don't worry. Many people will leave a gilt to 'run' with the boar and it will do him no harm if he is mature and there is space for the two animals to roam. However, with a young, inexperienced boar it can be stressful for him to be pestered by the sow.

Hogging and mating will last for two days. After this the sow will become uninterested in mating and will not 'stand' for the boar, who will in time cease to take an interest in her.

If you don't actually see the mating take

place, there are ways that you can check fairly reliably whether or not it has occurred. First, if sow and boar are running together, check them every day to see if they are staying close by one another; if they are, the chances are that she is ready to stand for the boar, and he will stay close to her for two to three days until she is no longer hogging.

Secondly, check the rear end of the sow – if a mating has taken place she will usually be a bit messy for several hours afterwards. The sow will often bunt the boar in the side with her head as if demanding his attention, and occasionally will let out a loud barking noise. The boar will also do this to the sow.

Another simple thing to look out for in wet weather is mud – if there is a lot of mud on the sow's back then it is fair to assume that the boar has mounted her. After a mating has taken place you may find a quantity of a jelly-like substance on the back end of the gilt or on the ground. This is the gel which seals the penis and cervix together to prevent contamination, and is often to be found after a mating has taken place.

However, if you see nothing at all, don't assume that nothing has happened – it usually does, so take a note of the date when you thought your sow was hogging, leave her in close proximity to the boar, then count on twenty days and watch to see if there is any reaction at all from the boar. If there is none then you can safely assume that she is in pig, although it is wise to keep an eye on her for several days after this date to be sure she doesn't return a little late. If there is a reaction, and she appears to be hogging again, repeat the whole process and wait another three weeks.

Mark the date of each service and the date the gilt is due to return (in season) on a calendar, even if you are fairly sure she is in pig; then check her at the time she would be due to come hogging again, as it is not unheard of for a sow to reabsorb her litter and return in season several weeks later. The reasons for this can be stress, or mild illness or infection, and it is similar to early miscarriage in humans. A sow can literally reabsorb the contents of her uterus and no foetuses will be expelled at all, so if this does happen you may not see any sign of it whatsoever.

Boar and sow can be left together following mating, and indeed up to the time when the sow is almost ready to farrow, if this is convenient for you. The boar will not trouble her, and she will be company for him.

Young boars should not be used more than once a week for stud purposes, although an older more experienced boar should be able to perform his duties once a day without any problem, and more frequently if he is rested in between matings (not left in with the sow).

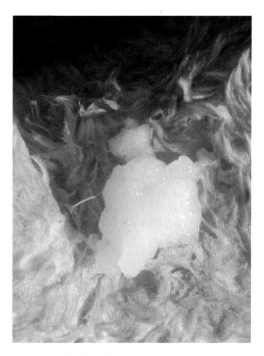

A large jelly-like plug may be found as a tell-tale sign that a mating has taken place.

A young, inexperienced boar may fail to get a sow pregnant for a variety of reasons, but with practice should master the task quite quickly. Remember that his sperm count will be low while he is immature, and give him the benefit of several failed attempts before condemning him. A boar should never be used for stud if he is under the age of seven months old. It is unusual, but not unheard of, for a boar to be infertile; however, infertility in a boar can be a temporary condition caused by environmental factors, such as excessive heat in the summer months, a minor infection which has caused him to have a temporary rise in temperature, and stress, injury or illness.

Never try to mate a young, inexperienced boar with a sow that is too large for him. Young boars need to be encouraged to do their job, and if they are discouraged by the difficulties of mating with a pig that is too big, or one that is not ready and is aggressive towards them, they can become impotent.

Young boars will occasionally show difficulties in covering their first gilt, so it is important to make it as easy as possible for them by putting them on level, dry ground without holes and slippery slopes, and by encouraging them to mount the correct end of the gilt. Avoid deep muddy paddocks, large stones on the ground, or anything else which could make it difficult or uncomfortable for the gilt to stand and for the boar to balance comfortably while mounted.

It will pay to help your young boar in the beginning – he will soon learn his task and will then be a lot more efficient and keen to work. An older, more experienced boar will usually get on with the task without any help needed.

When I have sows here for stud I always keep them for at least a further week beyond their return date (twenty-eight days from mating) before sending them home from the boar, as sometimes they can be a little late coming back into season. Twenty-four days after a successful mating, the eggs should have safely implanted in the uterus. If after two seasons the sow still returns (comes hogging again) and she is with a healthy, proven boar, then the chances are that she will not be going to conceive. In my experience this rarely happens, but of course it is always a possibility.

There are a couple of reasons for infertility in the gilt or sow: traditional breeds are at their breeding 'peak' at quite a young age, between twelve and eighteen months, and if they are not bred from then, the chances of them becoming barren (infertile) start to increase. A Kunekune gilt will be a little later, usually about two years, but will run to fat a lot earlier so it is important that she starts breeding by this age.

CHAPTER 4

GESTATION CARE

Gestation in pigs is 116 days – three months, three weeks and three days is an easy way to remember it. Once your mating has taken place and you are confident that it was successful, work out your farrowing date so that you may prepare everything in advance. Depending on how you work it out, the date may differ by a few days, so use both methods to calculate.

There are excellent breeding record books on the market (*see* Useful Addresses 'Supplies for Smallholders') and these are well worth having, as you can record the details of sow, boar, matings, expected date of delivery and all the necessary records for registering your piglets when they are born. The book will also hold details of when the birth took place, the number in the litter, and the details of each piglet born. These records are invaluable, not only for the current litter, but the next time that particular sow is in pig you can remind yourself of any complications there may have been (and possibly avoid them this time), how many piglets she had, and whether or not she was a productive mother.

You can also record any veterinary interventions or medicines that were necessary last time, and take appropriate steps to be well prepared this time. Finally, take note of any abnormalities, deformities, hernias and general health problems in your litters: this may help you to see where your problems are coming from, and perhaps if a pattern is forming between particular matings.

SIGNS OF PREGNANCY

If your gilt has been away to the boar for service, hopefully you will be able to rely upon the owner of the stud boar to tell you whether she is pregnant and exactly when to expect your litter to be born. They may even be able to scan her for you, in which case you will be able to relax and wait patiently for the first conclusive signs that your litter is on its way.

The first and most obvious sign that your pig is expecting a litter is her failure to return in season following her mating. Outward physical signs are not so obvious. Pigs can be scanned for pregnancy after the twenty-eighth day of gestation, although this must be done with a Doppler Ultrasound scanner as without Doppler the scanner may not penetrate the density of a pig's body mass. I have known a pig to be scanned with a basic ultrasound scanner, declared not in pig, and then to produce nine live piglets just over a week later!

A great deal depends on the type, breed and shape of your pig, but generally the first sign of a pregnant pig is the change in her teats. As she goes into the third month of her gestation you will probably notice that the teats are becoming more prominent. Her belly may also start to look a little round at this stage, and as her tummy swells and drops over the course of the following few weeks, the teats will begin to point out to the sides rather than downwards. Some sows will barely change shape at all until the final month, and at full term some will be very heavy, while in others the changes will be almost unnoticeable.

At the beginning of the fourth month – about three weeks before the piglets are due to be born – the vulva will start to increase in size. First it will appear puffy and engorged as it would when the sow is hogging, but it will continue to increase in size until the piglets are born, becoming quite slack and pronounced in the final stages of pregnancy.

At approximately two weeks before farrowing worm your gilt again; this will see her and her piglets through to weaning time.

FEEDING

Depending on the breed of pig and the individual sow, it may not be necessary to feed a sow any more during her pregnancy than you would normally feed her. What and how much to feed your pigs will vary from breed to breed, though by now you will probably have

ABOVE: A pig of correct weight, in healthy breeding condition.

OPPOSITE: An overweight pig. Carrying a burden of excessive weight will be detrimental to the health of the pig and will seriously compromise her chances of conceiving a litter.

established this; however, advice on the correct type of feed and the quantities to feed your sows is best sought from the breeder or supplier of your pigs.

Your aim will be to make sure that your sows maintain a healthy body condition score throughout their pregnancy. A sow that is fit is more likely to conceive and give birth to a healthy litter of piglets, and is less likely to have complications during her pregnancy or during farrowing; she will also produce plenty of milk to feed her litter.

A fat sow will not necessarily be 'doing' her piglets well in the womb, and will not be as able or energetic when it comes to farrowing: complications are more likely in a fat sow because she is likely to become exhausted more quickly, and will not be able to help her piglets out with good strong contractions. The longer a farrowing lasts the more stressful the experience will be for the piglets, and for the weakest this could be the difference between life and death. Furthermore sows that have endured a complicated or exhausting farrowing are more likely to require veterinary intervention, and to suffer post-farrowing complications, which may in turn lead to the cessation of milk production.

Condition scoring your sows is not difficult, and the table overleaf should be a good guideline to work to – though a heavily preg-

Condition Scoring Your Pigs

Description of Pig	Tail Area	Loins, Ribs and Flanks	Backbone
Emaciated Unacceptable	Deep cavity either side of tail, pin bones prominent	Ribs and pelvis obvious, hollow flank	Vertebrae obvious
Poor condition Unacceptable	Cavity around tail, pin bones slightly covered	Ribs and pelvis just covered, narrow flank	Vertebrae prominent
Slightly underweight Acceptable at weaning time	Pin bones covered and no cavity around tail	Ribs and pelvis covered but can be felt	Spine covered
Good, fit To be aimed for at all times	Pressure of the hand needed to locate pin bones	Ribs well covered, flank not hollow	Vertebrae only felt under pressure
Fat, overweight Acceptable at farrowing	Evidence of fat around base of tail	Ribs and pelvis cannot be felt	Vertebrae cannot be felt even under pressure
Very fat, obese Unacceptable	No room …	… for more FAT!	

nant sow will be a little more difficult to assess. Check her back fat and body condition by applying pressure with the flat of your hand to her spine, hips and pin bones on either side of her tail: this should give you a true measure of her condition.

Feeding 'by eye' is really the best way to learn to feed your pigs: like all animals, and people too, pigs vary in weight and metabolism. Some will utilize their food far more efficiently than others and therefore need less to eat; others will be more active and highly strung and will always seem to be a little on the lightweight side. Breeds such as the Mangalitza and the Kunekune are notoriously good 'doers' and will need very little extra feed.

Treat each pig as an individual during this important time, and if necessary separate your sows to feed them to ensure they get the correct ration to keep them in the best possible breeding condition. Sort the good doers from the not so good, and keep them in separate quarters so you can feed them appropriately.

If a sow is overweight and in pig through

the spring or summer months, it may not be necessary to feed her concentrates at all if she has access to good grazing. However, a good, balanced diet is essential.

Towards the end of the gestation period avoid increasing the ration of concentrates as this will encourage the growth of the already rapidly growing piglets. Large piglets are not necessarily healthier than their smaller counterparts, and are of course more difficult to push out, particularly for maiden gilts. Excessive feeding at this stage may also bring on mastitis (milk fever). However, in the last few days before the sow is due to farrow I would recommend gradually increasing the food ration by about 30 per cent, and feeding a little wet food. If you are using dry concentrates you could add a little water to make more of a mash, particularly if the sow does not have free access to grazing twenty-four hours of the day. A little oil in the feed is also acceptable in order to avoid constipation: a constipated sow will not be able to give birth to her litter without difficulty, and ideally she needs to clear her bowels in advance of the onset of her labour.

THE FINAL STAGES OF GESTATION

In the final week of gestation the udder will begin to form. The teats, now much larger than usual and quite prominent, will descend on the bottom of a sausage-shaped udder, which will be quite distinct from the rest of the belly: there is almost a ridge where the udder joins the lower belly. At this time, if you gently rub your hand backwards and forwards along the udder your sow should make lovely throaty grunting noises, and some sows will exhibit the same behaviour as when feeding a litter. I generally capitalize on this by making a lot of fuss of the sow in her

latter weeks, building a trusting relationship where I know she is relaxed in my company and is used to my being in close proximity to her nesting quarters, as well as becoming accustomed to my gentle handling of her.

If you handle your sow in this way each day you will notice the udder swelling as she approaches the birth date, and you may find that she is leaking a little clear fluid or even milk. In the final hours before farrowing, dark circles will appear around the teats, and the vulva will become larger and slacker at the end of gestation. At this time the birth is imminent and it is time to keep a close watch on your sow.

If the udder becomes hard and hot or seems uncomfortable for the sow, seek advice from your vet straight away as this may be the onset of mastitis and will need immediate treatment.

WORMING AND FINAL PREPARATIONS

Look out for mange and lice in your pregnant sows. An injection of an ivomec-based anthelmintic will treat lice and mange mites as well as internal parasites; if you have used an oral wormer then you may need to treat for lice and mange as well. This will ensure that your piglets are protected until weaning, and that there are no parasites present in the maternity ward! Internal and external parasites can really take their toll on young piglets, so it is important to be vigilant.

If you should need to restrain your pig for any kind of treatment when she is heavily in pig, try to do it carefully, causing as little stress as possible. Move her slowly from place to place. Do not travel your sow in the latter stages of her pregnancy: it is, at the time of writing, against animal health and welfare law to travel a sow when she is more

These three photographs show the gradual development of the udder during the final week of pregnancy. The first one shows the teat development and the udder beginning to form; the second shows good development of the udder; and the third shows the udder fully bagged up approximately twenty-four hours before farrowing.

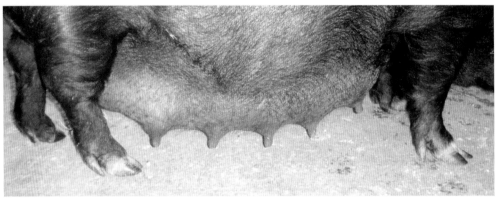

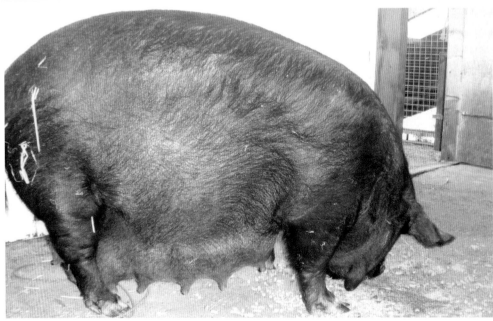

At the very end of gestation the vulva will become bigger and slacker.

It is important that your sow has a place to cool down in extremely warm weather.

than 90 per cent into her pregnancy (104 days). Travelling can be physically and mentally stressful for a pig, and should be avoided in the latter part of pregnancy.

Avoid contact with other pigs, except of course for her companion(s). Bear in mind that even a minor infection and any significant rise in body temperature during pregnancy can cause a sow to abort or to reabsorb her litter, with possibly no outward sign that anything is wrong.

If the birth is due to take place during hot weather it is most important to ensure the sow has constant access to a wet, muddy wallow, and even to gently trickle cold water over her if she appears distressed with the heat: start at the back and work forwards, though never pour water over her head. In the winter months it is equally important to ensure that she is warm and comfortable and has plenty of dry bedding.

I have noticed that some sows in the last couple of days of their pregnancy, will stay up very late at night contrary to their usual routine, grazing well into the early hours of the morning, almost as though they are 'stockpiling' food for the coming days when they won't feel much like getting up and leaving a newborn litter for more than a short period of time.

Seven days before the expected date of farrowing, settle your pig in the place where she is to have her piglets. My pregnant sows all live together until this time, but then I let the expectant mother roam free and shut her in her farrowing quarters at night. When first separated from her friends she may wander back to their gate during the day, but she quickly begins to enjoy her new routine, and appreciates a bed of her own when she is heavy and uncomfortable.

Moving her a little in advance of her due date will help her to get used to her new surroundings, and prevent any anxiety about being moved when farrowing is imminent, allowing her to settle well before she has her piglets. Once established in her quarters I will leave a low light on overnight so it is easy to pop in and check on her without disturbing her too much.

It is usual for the sow to farrow at around 116 days. If your sow goes more than seven days past her due date and you are sure that she was served on the date in your diary, get a vet to check her. However, if she is over a week late, it is more likely that your dates were wrong and that she will deliver three weeks later than expected, having been served on her following season.

Very occasionally a sow will deliver a day or two earlier than you expect.

When birth is imminent, the sow will begin 'nesting'.

IN CONCLUSION

Above all, throughout the gestation of the sow, remember that you are aiming for optimum health and condition. A fit, healthy, stress-free sow will be more likely to reward you with a good litter of healthy piglets and an udder full of milk with which to feed them!

CHAPTER 5

FARROWING

PREPARING THE FARROWING QUARTERS

The farrowing accommodation for your sow should provide a sheltered and draught-free environment, and it is vital to ensure that it is extremely clean: if it has housed pigs before, remove all bedding and disinfect where possible, leaving ample time for it to dry out thoroughly before your sow moves in.

An important consideration is space: always farrow your pig where there is room and light for you to see what is going on – a small pig arc in the middle of a field is not suitable. Remember that in the event of an emergency a vet may have to attend and he will need space and lighting to work. If you intend to use a heat lamp, which I strongly recommend, then you will also need electricity.

Many people farrow their pigs outdoors in a pig arc, away from the buildings, and offer no assistance or intervention at all. This is fine if you are prepared to accept losses as routine; indeed you may be lucky and wake up to find a healthy sow with a healthy litter – but there is no harm in being attentive and careful. Personally I look forward to, and enjoy, every farrowing and every litter as much now as I did with my very first, and would not miss it for the world. And quite apart from these sentiments, I know that I have saved countless piglets' lives and the lives of at least two sows by being on hand in an emergency.

The ideal place to farrow your sow is in a stable, barn or shed of some sort, which opens on to grazing or an outside foraging area. This can be adapted for purpose as soon as it is suitably disinfected and thoroughly dried out. A farrowing house with a door on it is ideal as there may be times when you need to put the sow out of the way for a few minutes in order to tend the piglets. This may be for the purpose of treating a poorly piglet, separating young boars for castration, or just for cleaning the bedding, but it will be very handy, particularly if your sow is very protective.

Be sure to be able to make your farrowing pen fox-proof at night as foxes will take newborn piglets from the sow.

Building a Creep

You will need to build a 'creep', an area that the piglets can access easily but where the sow cannot get in with them; however, it needs to be constructed so that she can see the piglets all the time. It is important *never* to feed piglets in the creep, as your sow will demolish it in order to 'steal' their food, and probably injure some of them in the process.

An ideal barrier would be a hurdle or gate, or some sturdy bars or poles situated vertically, or horizontally about 30cm (12in) off the ground, and high enough so that your sow cannot climb over them. Whether the bars are horizontal or vertical, they need to be close enough together – about 15cm (6in) – so that the sow cannot get her head between them and get it stuck.

Using a Heat Lamp

Place a heat lamp above the piglet area, taking care that it is high enough that neither piglets nor bedding can possibly be burned by it. Instructions to this effect are usually given on the box in which the bulb comes: on mine it says no less than 1m (39in), but these lamps do vary so be sure to check. Make sure that there is nothing close by which could fall on the lamp, or touch it and catch fire: hay, straw and cobwebs are particularly important. Make a soft bed of straw under the lamp; it does not need to be too deep, as the piglets will have the warmth from the lamp so will not need to bury themselves in the straw.

Bedding

The sow's quarters alongside the creep need to be bedded down with straw – though again, not too much straw prior to farrowing, and short straw is best as piglets can become tangled in long straw. The sow will need enough to make a comfortable nest, but you do not need a huge amount as the piglets may get buried in it and get trodden on. About half a small bale is sufficient, as you can top up the bed and make it more comfortable the day after farrowing, when the birthing process is over. Ensure that your straw is of good quality and not mouldy or dusty.

Never use sawdust or shavings in the farrowing area as these can be inhaled by the piglets and lead to chest problems. A light scattering of wood shavings or sawdust in the far corner of the farrowing quarters or wherever the sow chooses to make her toilet area is acceptable, as this will absorb the wet and will not come into close contact with the piglets.

Building a Crèche

If your piglets have access to the outdoors from an early age a crèche is a good idea: this is an area away from the farrowing quarters with access to the outdoors where the piglets can wander but cannot stray too far from safety. This is essential in areas with birds of prey, especially if the piglets are away from buildings or populated areas.

A crèche can be constructed of planks of wood about 15 to 20cm (6 to 8in) tall, high enough to keep small piglets in, but low enough for the sow to step over them and move away and graze alone. Some arcs are made with a detachable crèche, so if you are not using the arc for farrowing, you can detach the crèche and place it at the opening of your chosen farrowing area.

Ventilation and Draughts

Another word on arcs: should you choose to farrow your pig in an arc, make sure that there is sufficient ventilation for air to circulate. It is important to strike a distinction between draughty and well ventilated, as piglets are susceptible to chest problems, and

OPPOSITE: *Piglets safe and warm behind the bars of a simple home-made creep constructed from a firmly anchored sheep hurdle.*

If farrowing in a field situation, a crèche outside the arc will stop young piglets from wandering away but will allow the sow access to the field. (Courtesy Darrell Palmer-Swaine)

damp air or condensation will do them no good at all. A heavy plastic 'curtain' or a piece of carpet on the front door of the arc will keep out unnecessary cold and reduce draughts. Also, choose an arc fitted with farrowing rails, or which has a built-in farrowing 'lip': these will prevent the piglets from being trapped and squashed by the sow when she lies down against the side of the arc.

If your pig is farrowing in a large area – for example a barn or large shed – make the corner where she is bedded down as cosy as possible by placing bales around it; these will stop draughts, and will also prevent the piglets from wandering too far from their mother just after they are born. Leave a small opening between the bales, just large enough for the sow to come and go. (Do not, however, put these extra bales round the sow until she is well settled and past her nesting stage, or they will soon be ripped up and become part of the nest!)

The Provision of Water and Food

Fresh water must be available to the sow at all times. Make sure your water container is not deep enough for the piglets to drown in – buckets are definitely not a good idea, as a piglet several weeks old can easily tip head first into a bucket and will not be able to turn himself the right way up again.

A shallow trough or tray is best, and if it is any more than a few inches deep, put some bricks into it so that a piglet can keep himself out of the water should he accidentally stray into it. Replenish the water supply regularly so it is always fresh and clean. Piglets will start to drink water from about ten days onwards, so the water container must be accessible to them as well as their mother. Be sure that your container is firmly fixed or of the type that cannot be tipped over; a wet farrowing pen is a breeding ground for germs and bacteria.

If you are using a trough to feed your sow, be sure that it has no sharp edges and cannot be tipped over and injure the piglets. There are good rubber 'trugs' on the market now which are difficult to tip over and almost unbreakable so are ideal for this situation. Personally I prefer to feed my sows on a clean floor because the piglets will begin to eat solid food with their mother at about seven to ten days old, and if the food is on the floor they will be able to help themselves without getting too close to their mother while she is feeding.

Sows are particularly greedy when nursing a litter and will show no mercy when it comes to feeding time if the piglets are getting in the way! If you should decide to use a trough or feed bowl for the sow, spread a little extra food around the floor for the piglets.

NESTING

Once you have noticed some or all of the signs mentioned above in the final stages of gestation, nesting will follow. It is a good idea to wash the sow's udder with a mild disinfectant and warm water just before she farrows to prevent infection which could cause mastitis. Do this away from the nest to prevent the bedding getting wet.

Nesting is a wonderful time to quietly observe your sow at work. You and she will now be full of anticipation, and you will see a marked change in character in your gilt, from juvenile spoilt piggy to maternal introvert. The nesting instinct is very strong and is something which indoor sows in intensive pig units do not have the opportunity to fulfil. Be sure to give your sow the peace and quiet, space and materials to indulge her nesting instinct to her maximum potential!

I don't think I have ever seen a sow give birth without at least one hour of nesting, and sometimes as much as twelve hours. It can involve quite extreme behaviour, such as collecting all kinds of things and burying them in the bed – I have known grooming brushes, newspaper, a hosepipe, a broom, and even a log basket find their way into a sow's nest! She will usually grunt gently to herself while she is nest building, and will often stop to lie down and rest before beginning to rearrange the bed once again. She will collect her materials in her mouth and carry them around with her for some time, and will also dig the bed over gently with her trotters. And just when you think she is settling down for the birth, she will haul herself back to her feet and start all over again!

Nest building can continue right up to when the pushing begins, but usually there is a period of calm, almost sleep, before the birthing begins. At this time the sow's breathing may be laboured and erratic. Once she is settled at this stage it's a good idea to put the heat lamp on to warm the bedding and also to cast a gentle light around so you can see what's happening if it is dark.

Most farrowings seem to take place at night; I suspect this is an inborn instinct in the sow, like many other animals who like to give birth under cover of darkness when they feel they will not be disturbed.

Sow settled under a gentle light, pausing during nest building.

THE BIRTH

Generally pigs farrow without any difficulty, but it's always worth being there to help in the event of a problem; very occasionally a sow giving birth for the first time will take a while to settle down and will be up and down like a yo-yo for the first piglet or two. This can lead to piglets being trodden on or squashed under her weight, which is of course easily avoidable if you are there to keep an eye on her. If you find your sow is unsettled and getting up and down, quietly remove each piglet as it is born and put it under the heat lamp in the creep until she settles down again.

As long as you are a quiet observer, most sows will not mind you gently moving the piglets to one side where they are safe if she is a bit 'busy' to start with.

Labour will begin in its intensity with visible contractions which will build in strength for possibly about an hour before the first piglet is born. At this time you will probably see a discharge from the vagina which should be clear or pinkish but not bloody, and it may contain faeces from the piglets which will look like tiny black currants.

The time will vary hugely from one pig to another, and it is impossible to say what is 'normal'; in fact it is easier to discuss what is not normal.

A pig that has been pushing hard – so much so that her body is lifting slightly and her legs are raised – should not push for more than an hour without you seeing some progress towards a piglet being born. This may only be the appearance of the tips of trotters, but as long as things appear to be progressing you need not worry about the time involved. With first-time gilts a lengthy birth is only to be expected, but older sows will usually get going quite quickly once the pushing has begun. Remember to check your watch so that you know how long the sow has been pushing.

If you feel anxious and are concerned that things are not happening, it does no harm to ring the vet, tell them exactly what is going on, and see if they are concerned: they will advise you how long to wait, or they may come out and look at her if they think something is wrong. If you are at all worried, it will help to get their reassurance.

As the birthing progresses, most sows will enter an almost 'comatose' state: deep, laboured breathing is the norm, and apart from the occurrence of regular contractions, the sow will not move from her adopted position.

Unlike other animals, pigs do not turn round and clean off the piglets as they are born (indeed, just their physical make-up at full term would make this impossible without standing up) or guide them to suckle from the teat. With an air of determination to survive, all but the weakest of piglets will struggle to remove themselves from their little birth sac.

Most piglets are fairly active when they are born and will shake their heads vigorously, clear their airways and begin to breathe without any difficulty. As they are born you will notice that the umbilical cord will pump until breathing is established and the piglet becomes an independent being. There is no need to sever the cord, and nor does the sow do this: it will break quite naturally after the piglet is born.

Once breathing, he will begin the journey along his mother's belly to establish himself on a teat. Some piglets will wander away from the mother a little and will therefore lose the warmth from her body and can sometimes become disorientated. This is when your straw bales or crèche are invaluable, because if they were not there, the piglet might wander too far and perish in the cold.

A healthy newborn piglet. His umbilical cord is still thick and pumping and he has yet to shed his little birth sac.

Don't be tempted to remove the amniotic sac from the piglet when he is born: it will dry and peel away from the body gradually, thereby allowing the piglet time for his body temperature to adjust to the dramatic change from living inside the warm, watery belly of the sow to the distinctly chilly air in the world he has now entered. However, it is a good idea to gently remove the mucus from around his snout to ensure he can breathe freely.

As the piglets are born and latch on to a teat their suckling will in turn stimulate further contractions in the sow and the birthing process will continue. Some piglets will sleep after their birth and wake up to suckle some time later.

Farrowing can be a lengthy operation. However, once the pushing starts in earnest the piglets will appear at fairly regular intervals. A maiden gilt will of course take a little longer than a sow who has had several litters, but anything from a few hours up to a whole day is normal.

Unless you are very experienced, it is unwise to attempt to interfere with what looks like a difficult birthing – leave it to the vet or someone who knows what they are doing. Also some sows do not like being observed, and will literally hold on to the piglets despite strong contractions. If I suspect this is happening I will leave the sow in peace, just going back to check at regular intervals to see that everything is going smoothly and that the piglets are fine.

Some breeds are more relaxed than others, and depending on the temperament of your sow you may find it necessary to keep your distance and observe where she is unaware of your presence. In my farrowing barn I have set up a CCTV so I can watch what is going on without having to disturb the sow at all if she is not happy with an observer. I will only join her if I see a piglet born which looks as if it may need assistance. CCTV is also useful on those freezing cold nights in the winter when nothing happens for hours and hours: better to be watching from the warmth and comfort of your own bed than from the uncomfortable corner of a cold barn!

Some piglets will be born very weak – usually the last ones to be born, or occasionally the first born if it is a large piglet that has been stuck for some time in the birth canal. Weak piglets may need a little help to get them breathing. First, gently clear the mucus from the snout and mouth. If there is no breathing there are several methods you can try to get things going: a little piece of straw pushed very gently just inside the snout will sometimes start the piglet off by making him sneeze; or holding him upside down by his back legs and swinging him to and fro often works – but be sure to dry his legs first and get a firm grip on them, because you don't want to drop him on his head!

If all else fails, rub his chest gently – and as a last resort, mouth to mouth is sometimes successful. If you do administer mouth to mouth, blow very softly into the piglet's lungs – bear in mind how tiny they are, and keep your fingers round the chest cavity of the piglet so that you can feel when your breath is inflating the lungs.

Sometimes two or more piglets will be born in very quick succession. If this happens it is possible that the piglet at the bottom of the pile may suffocate if the piglet(s) on top doesn't move out of the way quickly, especially if he is small and weak. If you are in attendance, see that all piglets are free of obstruction and able to breathe within a minute or two of their birth. Some piglets may present themselves head first, and some will be breech – it seems to make little difference to the sow.

The uterus of a pig has two sides, or

'horns', as they are known. Each horn has the capacity to hold several piglets, although sometimes all the piglets will be on one side. Occasionally the piglets in one horn will have died and been reabsorbed, and sometimes they will be stillborn, but most often there will be live piglets born from both horns.

During a normal, straightforward birth there is generally a pause in the proceedings before the second side or horn is emptied. To the amateur pig man, this pause makes it seem as if the birth is complete, particularly as a little afterbirth will often appear before the next piglets are born. However, never be satisfied that a birth is finished until you have seen that the complete afterbirth has been expelled. It is often the last piglets that will need your help the most, as they have been on their journey through the birth canal for the longest.

It is vital that your pig expels her afterbirth within a few hours of the birth. Unlike some animals, pigs will contract infection from retained afterbirth very quickly, and this can result in the loss of your sow in extreme cases, and the cessation of the milk supply in less extreme cases. If you are in doubt as to whether your sow has 'cleansed' fully, be sure to administer an injection of oxytocin, which will assist the cleansing and 'closing down' of the cervix, and an antibiotic injection to prevent infection.

A small and weak piglet. He should be dried, warmed and supported until he is sucking well.

A complete afterbirth, carefully laid on a towel to show the shape of both horns of the uterus.

Oxytocin is a hormone injection which your vet may allow you to keep at home and administer yourself. 2ml injected into the rump or neck muscle with a long needle – approximately 5cm (2in) – should be sufficient to be sure to bypass the fatty layer and penetrate the muscle.

A Difficult Birth

In the event of a very difficult birth, internal examination and/or assistance may be necessary. However, never attempt to interfere with the birth unless you are confident that you know what you are doing. Cleanliness is of the utmost importance, and before undertaking an internal examination (if you feel able to do this yourself) remove any jewellery, wash your hands and arms with a mild disinfectant, be sure of clean short fingernails, and use a lubricating gel or mild soap suds.

Enter the sow very gently, and never push against her contractions. If you withdraw your hand, cleanse it again before re-entering her. If a piglet or piglets are stuck close to the exit, it may be possible, with extreme care, to gently release them. Never pull a piglet if the sow is not contracting: work with her and be very sympathetic and cautious, avoiding all possibility of a rupture. When conducting an internal examination you may not be able to feel any piglets at all if they are still deep inside the uterus. Sows, even small ones, have a huge uterine cavity.

If you are in any doubt, call out a veterinary surgeon to do this examination for you.

from their mother within the first twelve to twenty-four hours of life. After the first six hours of life the composition of the gut begins to change, and the ease with which the colostrum is absorbed also changes. After twenty-four hours the gut of the piglet will have 'closed down' its ability to absorb colostrum, and if the piglet has not had his fair share by this time he will be vulnerable to disease and viruses, and the development of his vital organs will be impaired.

The Effects of No Colostrum

Early studies showed the disastrous effects of having no colostrum, in that virtually all the piglets that were deprived of colostrum died before they reached 90kg live weight. There were many causes of death, but all related to an inability to resist trivial infections, either of the joints or of the respiratory and digestive systems.

(Pinder, Gill, 2002)

The Importance of Colostrum

Piglets that had intakes of colostrum within the first three hours of life had significantly higher IgG (Immunoglobulin G) blood levels at five days of age, compared with those piglets that were born after three hours. This shows the importance of sufficient colostrum intake in the first three hours after

(Eric van der Hoeven,
Colostrum: Let Them Drink!)

In short, the life expectancy of a piglet which has not had sufficient colostrum in the first twelve hours of its life will be much less than that of a piglet which has had a good share of colostrum.

Colostrum intake in piglets is highly variable and dependent on many factors. The minimum colostrum requirement for a piglet is not known, but suffice to say, the more the better, and adequate intake would be in the range of 200–450g (7–16oz) per piglet.

In a large litter the piglets will of course receive less colostrum than piglets in a small litter, and the weaker piglets in a large litter will be likely to go short as they will not be so capable of battling for their teat in the early stages. You can help these piglets (if your sow will allow it) by holding them on to a teat and supporting them whilst they drink.

You can also take colostrum from the sow – or another sow which has plenty – by milking her (if she will allow it) into a syringe and feeding it to the piglet by using a stomach tube. Warm the tube with very hot water to soften it so that it is easier to insert. Push it gently into the side of the mouth and down the throat of the piglet. Hold the tube high so that gravity will aid the milk flow. Gently pour the milk into the tube and allow the milk to drain into the piglet completely before swiftly withdrawing the tube.

This method is useful if the piglet is weak and will not suckle: it saves time and ensures the piglet has received the correct quantity. This practice is regularly used with lambs, so if you are not sure about it, a friendly sheep farmer should be able to help you out!

It may be necessary to take the stronger piglets away from the sow for a few minutes in order that the weaker ones can get plenty of suckling time. The stronger piglets will be quite all right if they are away from the others for five or ten minutes at a time, as long as they are somewhere warm. This may seem to be a lot of bother, but it should only be necessary for the first twelve hours or so, and it will be well worth it. Aim for 100 per cent survival rate in your litters, and you won't go far wrong!

IRON

Once you are sure that all the piglets are drinking, your next concern will be their iron intake. Piglets will follow their mother outside sometimes from as early as the first day. This is to be encouraged in good weather, but remember that piglets are vulnerable for some time and can fall prey to foxes, buzzards and other birds of prey, mink, and small animals such as polecats.

If the sow has farrowed in a barn or shed or similar, she should be given access to the outdoors as soon after farrowing as possible. She will probably bring in soil on her udder, which the piglets will absorb whilst nuzzling and feeding.

When the weather is fine and imposes no restrictions on the piglets, it is fascinating to see a sow take her new litter outside and leave them in what she considers to be a safe place while she goes about her business, then with one grunt at just the right pitch some time later, she will have them all running squealing towards her for the next meal!

Piglets born inside or without immediate access to the outdoors will require iron by injection or orally at approximately three days old. A simple injection into the muscle

Berkshire piglet rooting in the soil. Soil is the natural answer to iron intake in piglets.
(Courtesy Lucy Scudamore)

(neck or hind leg) will prevent anaemia. A needle of appropriate size should be used: 21 gauge/⅝in for small piglets. It should not be necessary to repeat this with outdoor-bred piglets as they should be outside nuzzling the soil within the first week, and will thereby take in further iron.

At birth a piglet will have a certain level of iron (haemoglobin) in its blood. However, its only immediate source of iron is its mother's milk, and sow's milk is deficient in iron. By approximately seven days of age the level of iron in the piglets' blood will start to drop, and by two to three weeks of age anaemia will set in. Signs of anaemia may be visible in piglets as young as seven to ten days old. There will be pallor in the gums and the mucous membrane around the eyes, and in severe cases the piglets may show signs of difficulty breathing, and may also scour.

When injected, an anaemic piglet may bleed profusely.

It is possible to treat anaemia, but it is far better to prevent it in the first place and save yourself the problems associated with this deficiency, which may also affect the growth rate of your piglets.

As a precaution against anaemia it is a good idea to put a mound of soil or a sod of turf inside the farrowing quarters or creep so that as soon as the piglets are up and about they can begin to nuzzle this.

HANDLING

Avoid handling newborn piglets if possible. On the occasions when you do have to handle them – for example, when spraying their navels or injecting them – do so with great care. The correct way to lift a young piglet is by its hind leg: it will be noticeably quieter when picked up in this manner than if picked up and cradled like a puppy or baby.

The correct way to handle young piglets is to hold them by the hind legs: they will be less vocal if handled in this way.

Be especially careful not to grab or squeeze piglets, as this can result in the development of a hernia.

Always try to do your necessary handling while the sow is otherwise occupied with her food, or is outside grazing, as this will avoid stressing her.

INJECTING

When medicines are prescribed by your vet there will always be instructions on the label as to how and in what quantity the substance should be administered. If you buy a product 'over the counter' then there will be instructions on or inside the packaging.

If an injection is to be given intramuscu-

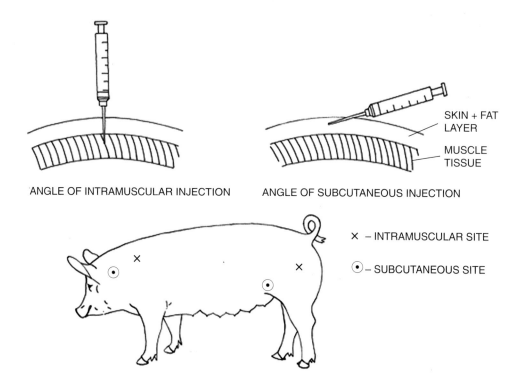

ANGLE OF INTRAMUSCULAR INJECTION   ANGLE OF SUBCUTANEOUS INJECTION

SKIN + FAT LAYER

MUSCLE TISSUE

× – INTRAMUSCULAR SITE

⊙ – SUBCUTANEOUS SITE

The correct sites for injecting pigs.

larly, it can be given into the neck muscle or the hind leg muscle: inject at right angles to the pig, directing the needle straight in. If it is to be given subcutaneously (under the skin) it should be given behind the ear or into the skin of the stifle at the top of the hind leg: inject at an angle of 45 degrees. (*See diagram above.*)

Always dispose of needles after a single use, as a dirty or blunt needle can cause an abscess to form at the injection site. It is best to have an assistant to hold the piglet for you whilst you inject: this will make the process quicker and easier for both you and the piglet.

FEEDING

It should not be necessary to feed creep food to your piglets whilst they are still feeding from their mother; however, be sure to feed your sow well whilst she is producing milk for her litter – after a 'settling in' period of twenty-four hours after the birth, you can start to gradually increase the sow's intake of sow nuts.

Feed quantities will vary according to the breed and size of the sow. As a rule of thumb, by the time the litter reaches three weeks of age, their mother will be eating 3kg (6lb) of food for herself and 0.5kg (1lb) of food for each piglet that she is feeding – thus a sow feeding a litter of eight piglets will be eating 6kg (14lb) of food per day. The exceptions to this rule are the small breeds such as the Kunekune and Pot Bellied pigs. These little pigs will need approximately ½kg (3lb) of food for the sow and ¼kg (½lb for each piglet

Young piglets learning to forage by copying their mother; they will start to eat her food at about seven to ten days old.

she is feeding – thus a sow feeding a litter of eight piglets will be eating 3kg (7lb) of food a day.

The protein level of the food is also important: big, traditional sows will need approximately 16–18 per cent protein in their feed, while the smaller Kunekune or Pot Bellied pig will need no more than14–16 per cent.

The piglets will begin to help themselves to the sow's food by the time they are approximately seven to ten days old.

Keep a close eye on the weight of your sow: some sows will 'milk off their backs' and lose weight dramatically while feeding a litter. If you think your sow is losing weight, in-crease the food ration again until you are happy that her weight remains stable.

By the time the piglets reach weaning age (at approximately eight weeks) they will be helping themselves to a considerable amount of their mother's food and will be well accustomed to 'hard' feed, ready for the transition at weaning. At weaning you may increase the protein ration for traditional weaners to 18–21 per cent. With the smaller breeds it is best to decrease the protein ration to 12–14 per cent, but it is important that the piglets are reared on pig food as they will need the vitamins and minerals in a pig food ration to help them develop and grow.

CLEANLINESS

Cleanliness is of the utmost importance with a new litter. Clean any dung from the bedding each day, remove any wet straw, and clean the floor as best you can without washing it down.

If your sow is particularly protective, you can still do this while she is busy eating her food, as long as care is taken. Piglets are prone to respiratory problems, and wet, cold bedding is likely to encourage this.

CASTRATION

If you are intending to rear your boar pigs for meat it will be uneconomical and unnecessary to castrate them. However, if you are rearing them as pet or companion pigs, then castration is essential. Remember that it is your responsibility as the breeder to castrate your boar piglets, and you should not pass on this task to the person who buys them.

Please remember that full boars must never be sold as pet pigs.

If you intend keeping a boar back to use for stud, seek advice on keeping the right one. At such an early age it is very difficult to tell – unless you are experienced – which pig will be no better than mediocre, and which – if indeed any – will be outstanding. With the Kunekune, many people are seduced by colour and think they have a boar piglet worth keeping just because his coat is a beautiful colour. Sadly he may well grow into a pig that is not really good enough to be bred from.

If you are keeping a boar piglet back to sell on for breeding, be prepared to keep him for at least twelve months, as many people will not want to buy a boar unless he is proven as a stud. If you should sell him any younger than this and he should turn out to be infertile, it is your responsibility as the breeder to refund or replace him.

It is a good idea to talk to your vet about this subject before your piglets are born: find out what his preferences are on the matter, and plan accordingly. Some vets prefer to do this operation at a very early age – my own vet likes me to take the piglets into the surgery at about ten days old, while others prefer to wait until they are about four weeks of age. Castration can in fact be performed at any age, but the risks to the pig are far greater when he is several months old, and of course the cost will be far greater for an older pig.

I consider it best practice to take the piglets into the surgery, away from the sow, for this procedure; if done at home it can be very distressing for the mother as it will be difficult to get her out of earshot, and there will be a good deal of screaming, simply because piglets do scream when handled. If you pack them all into a dog cage or some other similar transport which can be disinfected prior to, and following use, take them into the surgery and return them later to their mother: she will be none the wiser. The following are a few helpful hints:

- Take bedding from the creep to put in the carrier as it will smell familiar to the piglets
- If there is only one boar piglet that you wish to castrate in the litter, take another piglet along for company – it is stressful for the little one to travel alone
- When you return the piglets to the mother, put them back into the creep with the other piglets straightaway so they quickly lose any of the 'alien' smells from the vet's surgery, and watch to see the sow's reaction to the piglets. Be sure to watch that she feeds them all without any problem

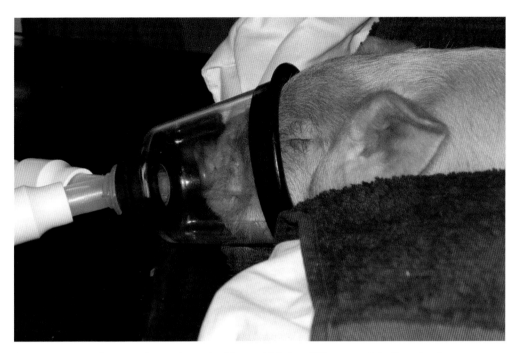

Castration operations can be performed with gas. This is a little more risky than local anaesthetic so the piglet should be closely monitored.

Castration should be a straightforward operation, taking no more than five to ten minutes as long as there are no complications. The scrotum will be cut, the testicles pulled out and removed, and a little antiseptic spray put on to the wounds. This can be done with local anaesthetic or with gas; there is slightly more risk with gas, and the piglet's heart rate and pulse will be monitored throughout the operation.

Closed Castration

Scrotal or 'inguinal' hernias are fairly common in pigs, and this problem can complicate castration. A 'closed castration' can be performed where there is a history of hernia in the breeding and this may solve the problem, although in extreme cases it will not. Ask your vet about this before your piglets go in for castration.

I have a closed castration operation on all my boar piglets as the Kunekune pig has a larger inguinal ring than other breeds of pig and is therefore predisposed to the problem of hernias. In these piglets it is often the presence of the testicles which is preventing the gut from protruding through the inguinal ring into the scrotum, and by castrating the piglet, this 'preventative plug' – the testicle – is removed, thus allowing the hernia to develop. In 'closed castration' the inguinal ring is sealed off with sutures, which should prevent the development of the hernia.

In extreme cases there will still be a problem and the only alternative to euthanasia will be a full scale, abdominal hernia operation where a 'mesh' or 'gauze' is inserted into

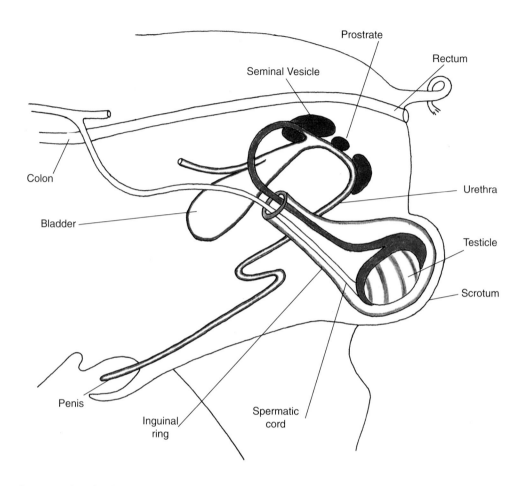

Cross-section drawing of the male pig showing the route of descent of the testicle through the inguinal ring.

the abdominal cavity to repair the damage. This is a lengthy operation which by its very nature has additional risks, but it is usually successful. It is, of course, relatively expensive, but if it provides the pig with a healthy and comfortable life thereafter, it is, in my opinion, worthwhile.

TEETH AND TAILS

I hardly feel I need to mention this in a book specifically written for the outdoor pig

breeder, who will treat his herd with respect and sympathy and will see that they are reared in a stress-free environment – but it is a question which I get asked surprisingly frequently: 'Should the teeth and tails of our piglets need cutting?'

Tooth clipping is done to prevent piglets from (a) face biting and (b) damaging the sow's udder. Both of these problems will occur particularly in large litters, whilst piglets are fighting to establish themselves on a teat. In intensively farmed pigs, the litters pro-

> Tooth clipping is likely to be very painful. The damage caused to the teeth is also likely to make them prone to infection.
>
> (*Compassion in World Farming 2010*)

duced are often extremely large, which in turn exacerbates this problem. In outdoor reared, natural pig breeding, litters are rarely excessively large, and the teats and milk produced are adequate for the size of the litters produced – another reason to be sure to select gilts for breeding carefully checking they have a sufficient number of good, evenly spaced teats.

If fighting at feeding time is excessive the sow will roll on to her tummy and prevent the piglets from feeding. She will rarely tolerate this behaviour, and will cease feeding them until the fighting stops. She will then resume her position and will allow the piglets to feed.

In outdoor herds where the piglets and sow can perform their natural behaviour patterns these problems will correct themselves without the intervention of man and his tooth clippers! Damage will only occur on rare occasions, and will need treating with antibiotic spray or disinfectant.

If fighting is prolonged and persists, then it is possible that the sow is for some reason not producing sufficient milk and the piglets are hungry, and further investigation will be necessary.

Tail docking is another practice applied to intensively reared piglets. Piglets that have no stimulation – no space to roam, ground to root in, straw to chew on – will turn to tail biting to vent their frustrations.

Recent science shows that the proper way of preventing tail-biting is to keep pigs in good condition, and not to dock their tails.

> Tail-docking has been proven to be extremely painful, not only when it is done but for some considerable time afterwards. It can also lead to abscesses forming on the spine...
>
> The problems of injury following tail-biting should be solved by improved management rather than by tail-docking.
>
> (*European Commission's Scientific Veterinary Committee (SVC).*

IN CONCLUSION

There are a few golden rules of piglet care, which I will again stress:

- Never pick piglets up (unless this is necessary for veterinary treatment or suchlike) as they will squeal very loudly, which will distress their mother
- Always treat a sow with respect – some are extremely amenable and long-suffering with visitors to their young, but don't upset them with enthusiastic children and noisy adults too soon. It is too much to expect of any new mum and can lead to distress, aggression, rejection of the litter and possibly even cannibalism
- Handle new-born piglets with great care. If handling is necessary, remember rough handling can cause hernias

CHAPTER 7

HAND REARING

In some cases it is necessary to hand rear piglets, although I stress that this should only be done as a very last resort. Piglets will always do better if they are on their mother's milk rather than artificial substitute milk, and will most often have a better chance of survival if they are in the litter rather than kept alone. I have hand reared piglets in the past which have looked as though they were at the point of giving up. In a final attempt to get some positive reaction from a non-suckler I have put him back with his mother and the rest of the litter, and have been amazed to hear him 'talk' to the others and try to take up his place alongside them at feeding time. He may not have been strong enough to drink, and I have had to continue substituting his milk supply, but his instinct to survive was still there, although only the presence of his siblings and mother could stir it.

Hand rearing piglets is rewarding, but not easy. Getting them to suckle is relatively easy, but that is the smallest and simplest of a long succession of hurdles for you and your 'orphans' to overcome. In the event that you lose your sow you will have to foster your piglet on to another sow (see 'Fostering' below) or hand rear. If at all possible, leave the (deceased) sow with the piglets as she will (hopefully) be full of colostrum and the piglets will be able to drink this: without it they will be facing an uphill struggle for life. Substitute colostrum is available on the market, but it is never as good as the real thing.

FOSTERING

If you can possibly foster your orphaned piglets on to another sow, this will give them the best possible chance of survival.

When fostering, the age difference between the orphan piglets and the piglets of the foster mother is important, as the composition of the mother's milk will change as her piglets grow. Newborn piglets fostered on to a sow with a week-old litter will not receive colostrum from this mother so they *must* be given colostrum from an alternative source.

In my experience, sows will take on foster piglets without much trouble as long as the litter is still kept to a reasonable size (no more than eight on a small sow, or ten on a large sow) so there is no fighting during feeding. If you can foster piglets on to a sow that is giving birth, the process will be easier: rub the orphan piglets in the birth fluid of the farrowing sow so they have the same scent as the newborns, but do not allow the orphans to steal the colostrum – be sure the newborns receive their fair share.

Timing is of the utmost importance with fostering: too early and you may deprive the newborn litter of their teats and colostrum, too late and the hierarchy will be established and the unused teats will be dry. However, if the sow is productive and takes well to the piglets, she will in due course produce milk from the initially dry teats if the piglets persist in suckling – though you may need to help them along for some time until she does produce more milk for them.

Older orphans that have been hand reared will soon learn to 'rob' milk from unsuspecting sows if they are allowed to run with other litters.

WHICH MILK AND HOW OFTEN?

Piglets can be reared on a variety of different milks. The best solution is sow milk replacer as this has been carefully formulated to be as close to the milk of a sow as possible. It is obtainable from good farm supplies shops and on the internet (*see* Useful Addresses); it does come in large bags but is worth it even if it only saves the life of one of your piglets.

To my mind, economy is not really a concern when hand rearing. If you do your sums and take into account the time and effort involved when hand rearing, it could never be very economical, but the rewards of successful hand rearing to a devoted pig keeper are plentiful and will far outweigh any financial rewards.

Goats' milk is easily digestible, although it is not really rich enough for piglets. I have used, with success, human baby milk for piglets; I tend to use 'follow on' milk for 'hungry babies' rather than the milk produced for newborns. This comes in small, airtight containers so it is easy to keep a tin for emergencies.

Newborn piglets will need to be fed once every hour for the first twenty-four hours. The quantity at each feed will vary with the size of the piglets, but a rough guide would be 20ml for a piglet weighing approximately 0.9kg (2lb). At two days old, piglets that are feeding well can be left for two hours between feeds, but those that are not should stay on the hourly feeding regime until a good feeding

Piglets will soon learn how to 'steal' milk from an unsuspecting sow!
(Courtesy George and Dani Clarke, Hi-Key Studios)

pattern has been established. By seven days old feeding can be reduced to every four hours, and a little longer overnight.

The more regular, small feeds you can give to your piglets, the better they will do, and once you have them lapping from a tray the whole feeding process will become far easier for you.

HOW TO FEED

If a piglet is too weak to suckle you can give him his first milk with a stomach tube. Alternatively, a small syringe or dropper can be used as long as the piglet's swallowing reflex is working. If the piglet is swallowing, he can be given 'piglet kickstart' or similar, a remedy full of iron, vitamins and essentials to build up strength. (*See* 'Equipment', Chapter 5.)

If your piglet is suckling it should be fairly easy to get him on to a bottle: an ordinary baby bottle is fine, and ordinary baby teats are about the right size for most piglets. Kitten and puppy teats and bottles are available for tiny piglets. (*See* Useful Addresses.)

One of the biggest difficulties to overcome that I have found with hand-reared piglets is teaching them to eat off the floor or out of a trough. If piglets are with their mother and siblings they will soon copy mother and start to forage with her when she eats. If hand reared they quickly become accustomed to their food being administered to them from 'above', rather than having to put their heads down to forage.

In order to avoid this problem it is important to get the piglet lapping from a tray on the floor as early as possible; once you have got milk into your piglet and he is eager to drink and has a healthy appetite you will need to starve him for a little while – half a day should be enough – and then give him his milk in a tray or low-sided dish on the floor. When there are several piglets present this works well, because at least one piglet will catch on quite quickly and the others will soon follow its example. One piglet on its own can take a little longer, but if you persevere, hunger will overcome!

Iron and Vitamins

Orphaned piglets will need their iron intake, and I would definitely inject all orphans, even those with access to the outdoors. A multivitamin injection such as Vitesel will also be a great help with orphans and a booster to their immune system development.

COMPLICATIONS ASSOCIATED WITH HAND REARING

It is not unusual for hand-reared piglets to 'fit' after feeding. They will sometimes take milk into the lung when drinking from a bottle or tray, and this causes a temporary loss of consciousness. Whilst this in itself is not harmful, the milk in the lung may be. Fluid of any type in the lung can become infected, resulting in pneumonia, which can be deadly in piglets.

This is a difficult problem to avoid, and the best advice I can give is to keep a strict eye on the piglets' breathing and at the first sign that something is not right, treat them with antibiotics. Sometimes you will be able to hear the fluid 'rattling' in the lung before the piglet shows any signs of ill health, and you may also notice the ribcage moving 'double time' when it is breathing.

Scouring (Severe Diarrhoea)

Scouring is common amongst piglets. Hand-reared piglets will have a lower immunity threshold to disease than piglets reared by their mother, so scours is more likely to be a problem. Treat early with antibiotics and ensure that the piglet does not become dehydrated: keep the fluids going in, and if scouring is severe, replace milk with rehydration fluid. This can be bought from your vet or farm supplies shop, but you can also mix your own, to the following recipe: 8 teaspoons of sugar, 1 teaspoon of salt, 1 litre of water.

Although it is difficult to avoid scours, cleanliness will help. Always keep the piglets' quarters as clean as possible, and sterilize feeding equipment if rearing piglets by hand. Be sure that trays, bottles and teats are kept as clean as possible.

Cross-contamination in a litter of orphans will be unavoidable, so any problems may well go through the whole litter. Sometimes you can avoid the spread of disease with preventative antibiotic treatment, so seek advice from your vet.

Note that it is advisable to give a probiotic to baby animals that are being treated with antibiotics: this will help to maintain the good gut flora, as these will be eradicated along with the bad if treatment with antibiotics is prolonged. Piglets love yoghurt, and live organic yoghurt is a good probiotic for any baby animal; a couple of teaspoons per piglet per day will suffice.

Constipation

Constipation is less likely to occur, but should this be a problem, a tiny amount of liquid paraffin – about 1ml – administered gently through a small syringe should sort it out.

Avoid diet changes if possible; if a change of milk or diet is necessary, introduce the 'new' gradually, mixing it with the 'old' before phasing this out completely.

Take Heart!

Colds, coughs, sickness and scours are all fairly common in animals with a very low immune system, but with each infection your piglets survive their immune system will strengthen, so you should take heart from this.

BODY TEMPERATURE

It is of course important to keep your piglets warm, and you should try to keep them at a fairly stable temperature. Piglets cannot control their body temperature at all, so in extremely warm weather they will quickly overheat, and in cold weather their body temperature will drop rapidly. A pig's normal temperature is 38°C.

An easy way to tell if your animal is too hot or too cold is to feel its ears, as these are a good indicator of overall body temperature. If a piglet has a cold mouth he will need warming up quickly – a cold mouth indicates a very low body temperature. A heat lamp or heat pad is the best way to keep the temperature stable in cold weather, but beware of piglets chewing electric cables.

In hot weather, make sure that piglets have access to fresh drinking water, shade and cool mud at all times. If a piglet appears to have overheated – and pigs do suffer from heatstroke – bring his temperature down by wrapping him in damp towels and putting vinegar behind his ears. Do not immerse him in cold water as this will be too great a shock to his system; however, it will help to gently trickle lukewarm water over him, starting at the back end and taking care to avoid his head and ears.

CHAPTER 8

WEANING

Weaning is best done at about eight weeks of age although there are exceptions; for example, if your sow is feeding a litter of more than eight piglets you may decide to wean at about six weeks if she is particularly underweight. If some of the piglets in the litter are a lot smaller than others it is acceptable to take the larger ones off at seven weeks and leave the smaller ones for another week to catch up. You will be surprised how quickly the little ones will put on weight if they don't have to compete for the milk with their larger siblings. (If using this method of weaning, do keep a check on the udder as there will be some teats which will not be used and the build-up of milk in them may cause mastitis.)

Weaning is an important stage in the development of your piglets and it is essential that it is done correctly to prevent stress to the piglets and difficulties with your sow. It is always best practice to take the sow from the litter rather than the other way around, so when arranging your farrowing quarters bear this in mind; what you are aiming for is an arrangement where it is simple for you to remove the sow and keep the piglets enclosed for at least seven days after weaning.

In the wild, a sow will gradually wean her piglets off milk at around twelve to fourteen weeks of age; by sixteen weeks they will be entirely independent of her. If you could watch this happen, you would see that the sow physically distances herself from the litter in stages, spending less time feeding them and sleeping with them as they become more mature and independent of her. Unfortunately, the way in which we generally keep our pigs does not allow this to happen, since most of us provide our sows with an enclosed paddock, a good shelter and/or possibly even shut them into a barn at night with their piglets.

When I have allowed my sows the freedom to show me how they would naturally wean their own litter, they have followed a pattern quite the opposite to the one I had always obliged them to follow. As weaning approaches at about six to eight weeks of age, my sows are normally wandering free with their piglets over many acres of ground. Through the day they will leave their piglets for increasing intervals between feeds, and the feeding time itself will become noticeably shorter, sometimes only lasting for a couple of minutes from start to finish.

For their own comfort and safety, I habitually confine sow and piglets to a barn or paddock at night where they are effectively 'trapped' together – but when I have observed them through the night, the sow is sleeping a considerable distance from the piglets, away from the nest, in order to rest peacefully, free from the demands of greedy mouths. It is interesting to observe that when allowed complete freedom to roam at this stage in the rearing of the litter, the sow would leave the piglets to sleep alone for the entire night, only returning to give them a brief feed first thing in the morning, then resuming her distancing from them throughout the day. This 'natural' weaning process is, of course, a much easier adjustment for sow and litter. However, for most of us it is not possible to follow this procedure.

FEED AND FEEDING

The piglets can now have their feed rations increased, in the case of small breeds (Kunekune and Pot-Bellied) to approximately ½kg (1lb) of pig food per piglet per day, and 1kg (2lb) for traditional breeds. For the latter, this feed ration should increase with age – approximately ½kg (1lb) of food for each month of age as a general rule: thus a three-month-old piglet will be eating 1.4kg (3lb) of feed, and a four-month-old 1.8kg (4lb). The Kunekune and Pot-Bellied should not need an increase in their feed ration, and ½kg (1lb) per day should be sufficient to rear them on.

Feed piglets twice a day at this age, and if they can have access to grazing, hay, haylage or similar, so much the better. There are other foods that are good for weaners, including maize, sugar beet and rolled barley, although pig nuts are the easiest method and of course contain all the nutrients necessary for growing piglets. Even if using some of these other foods, I would advise that 50 per cent of their daily intake should be pig food in order to ensure healthy growth and development.

Fodder beet is an excellent feed for piglets – even tiny piglets still with their mum will enjoy munching on fodder beet. I usually smash one with a sledgehammer so there are some small pieces that little piglets can manage. This also helps to occupy their time if they are shut in away from mother for weaning.

POST-WEANING CARE

The piglets should quickly adjust to life without their mother under these circumstances: they will be in familiar surroundings, with their siblings, familiar bedding, smells and comforts, all of which will reduce the chances of them suffering from post-weaning stress-related problems.

Problems you may encounter post weaning can include scouring (severe diarrhoea), loss of appetite, loss of condition and mange. All these conditions are relatively easy to treat, and should be quickly overcome if the piglets are weaned in the manner described above.

I will emphasize here that it is bad practice to sell piglets 'off the sow': it is unfair on the piglets and extremely unfair on your customers – many of whom may be first time or inexperienced pig keepers – to pass on the possibility of post-weaning stress-related problems to them. Always be sure to have your piglets in excellent condition before passing them on to new homes.

As soon as your piglets are weaned, worm them with an Ivermectin-based injection. It is particularly important to use this injection for worming at weaning time as many piglets do show signs of mange at weaning. Mange may lie dormant in your sow and may not become apparent in any of the piglets until they are weaned. It will manifest itself shortly after weaning in the form of sore or rough skin, a staring coat, and reddening around the hind legs, chest, ears and tummy: these symptoms will quickly worsen and the piglet will then start to lose condition, its coat will become

Big, chubby Kunekune weaners: shiny, healthy and ready for new homes. (Courtesy George and Dani Clarke, Hi-Key Studios)

'sticky' and dull, and thick scabs will start to form.

Vaccinations may also be given at this time, the most common being against erysipelas and parvovirus.

Two weeks after weaning your piglets should be fit, healthy, plump and shiny, and ready to start life in their new homes.

CARE OF THE SOW POST-WEANING

Once the sow is taken from her piglets, reduce her feed rations to the quantity that you would feed her when she is not feeding a litter. This reduction in protein will reduce the likelihood of her contracting mastitis. Try to put her where she is out of earshot of her piglets, and certainly where she cannot see them – any contact at all with them will encourage her to keep producing milk.

Check her udder after twelve hours and if it is hard, return her to the litter for one more feed; then remove her again straight away. It should not be necessary to do this more than

once. If hard lumps can be felt in the udder or the sow is uncomfortable, snappy, or unwilling to feed the piglets, treat her for mastitis with antibiotics and anti-inflammatories. If her udder remains large but soft, you can ignore it.

If your sow is in good condition post weaning, there is no reason why you cannot return her to the boar for service straight away. She should show signs of hogging within seven days of weaning, although there is no hard and fast rule to this and every sow is different. My personal belief is that when a sow is in the correct physical condition to conceive a healthy litter, she will return in season. Sometimes this is one week, sometimes it is several months, but generally in the first season after weaning your sow will be very fertile and will conceive a good litter.

If your sow is in poor condition post weaning and does come hogging right away, it is best to leave her until her second season. Follow the rules for 'flushing' in Chapter 3.

CHAPTER 9

PROBLEMS

PIGLET PROBLEMS

Check your piglets regularly: their first week of life is crucial, and you will learn a great deal from observing the litter. People often say 'Piglets are such a timewaster – I'm out there all the time!' – but this time isn't wasted: watching their habits, their position at feeding time, the way they breathe, the pecking order (which will begin at a couple of hours old) and the way they sleep, which ones are growing fast and which are not, will help you to identify problems very early on. And the earlier you identify problems, the more likely you will be to solve them. Indulge yourself in piglet watching – it is part of your job as a pig breeder!

Selenium Deficiency

Symptoms: Listlessness, respiratory problems, buckling of the back legs when walking, loss of condition followed by death.

Treatment
If you are in an area in which the soil is selenium deficient, I would recommend injecting your piglets with selenium and vitamin E. Selenium deficiency is a problem which manifests itself in sheep and lambs so you can find out by asking a local farmer.

Selenium and vitamin E are of vital importance in developing a good immune system, and until I became aware of the deficiency in our area, I lost many piglets to what we thought was common pneumonia. After many needless losses, we had one disastrous litter where four piglets were seriously ill. All were treated with several antibiotics, to which none of them responded. After the first death we had a post mortem performed, and followed it up with another when the second died two days later. Selenium and vitamin E deficiency was found to be the cause and all the other piglets were injected immediately. They all recovered, literally overnight, and thankfully we have not lost another one with this problem since.

Some sows and gilts are particularly deficient in selenium themselves, which naturally exacerbates the problem in their litters. Others, it seems, can get away with it, although I firmly believe that prevention is better than cure – so knowing that we have a deficiency in our area, I treat every litter without fail.

Anaemia/Iron Deficiency

Symptoms: If piglets are suffering from anaemia they will become weak and listless at about two to three weeks of age. They will be unthrifty and will lose condition, and will eventually die.

Treatment
Iron must be administered promptly, either by injection or orally. Once anaemia has set in, treatment by injection is essential as oral treatment may be slow to take effect.

To prevent iron deficiency, inject with iron at twenty-four to forty-eight hours old, and make sure piglets have access to soil or turf from the third day.

Atresia Ani (Blind Anus)

Symptoms: Some piglets are so tiny that it is difficult to check whether or not they have an anus without the help of a powerful torch.

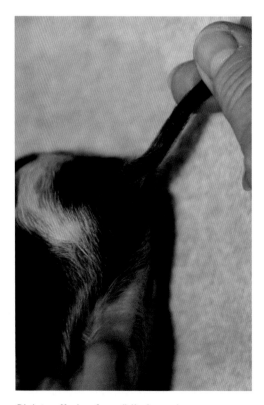

Piglet suffering from 'blind anus'.

This condition is difficult to spot until the piglet has fed well, when it will develop a round tummy. After a minimum of twenty-four hours it may show signs of discomfort, and the size of its tummy will increase rapidly. If untreated it may develop septicaemia and die.

This is a congenital deformity that only occurs occasionally.

Treatment
Surgery is the only treatment for this problem. Very occasionally it can be rectified by a small incision under the tail, although in my experience this is very distressing for the piglet. Furthermore often the colon is not properly developed, in which case nothing can be done to help the piglet and euthanasia is the only option.

There are variations on this problem: sometimes the piglet will be seen to defecate and urinate through the vulva, and indeed I have known piglets such as this to survive for many months. However, they usually suffer from scours, urinary tract infections, and other related problems. Needless to say, they must not be bred from under any circumstances.

Oxygen Deprivation

Symptoms: Occasionally a piglet can be seen to spin in circles. If the problem is severe, the umbilical cord may be heavily tangled in straw soon after the birth.

Piglets suffering from this complaint will often be small and 'runty' as they have difficulty finding a teat and challenging other piglets for a place at the udder.

Treatment
There is no treatment as such, because this condition is the result of oxygen starvation at birth; depending on the severity of the prob-

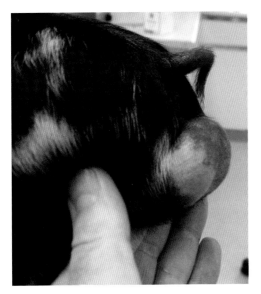

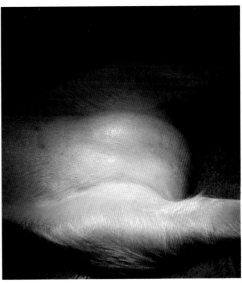

Piglet with a scrotal hernia. (Courtesy Dominic Alexander, MRCVS, Belmont Vets, Hereford)

Piglet with a scrotal hernia in position ready for his operation. Here you can see the extent of the bulge in his abdomen from the hernia. (Courtesy Dominic Alexander, MRCVS, Belmont Vets, Hereford)

lem, it may right itself in time. If you have a circling piglet be sure to keep an eye on him: his umbilical cord may get tangled in straw and can rupture, he may inadvertently wander away from the warmth of the nest and his mother, and he may also have difficulty finding his way to the teat and back to the creep.

If you help him along for a few days he will get stronger and the problem will usually disappear, although it will occasionally reoccur under stress.

Hernia

Hernia is a fairly common problem in piglets. There are three different types of hernia: diaphragmatic, scrotal (inguinal) and umbilical (abdominal). Scrotal and umbilical hernias are the most common.

A hernia occurs when part of the abdominal tissue that acts as a 'corset' becomes weak, and due to internal pressure develops a rupture. Pressure in the abdominal cavity pushes internal organs, and in particular the intestines, through the ruptured part of the abdominal tissue. This is manifested as a bulge, its size depending on how much of the organs have passed through.

Hernias are usually passed on in the breeding, although they can also be caused by rough handling, particularly around the hip area where unnecessary pressure can cause a scrotal hernia. Other contributory factors can be huddling together for warmth, and undue stretching of the umbilical cord.

Symptoms: Hernias are usually quite visible on a young piglet, although as the piglet grows they may become more difficult to spot; on the other hand they may get considerably larger.

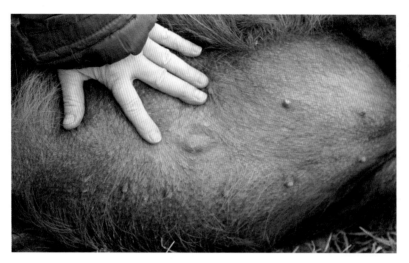

An umbilical hernia on a nine-month-old gilt pig. This gilt should never be bred from.

A scrotal hernia can be seen quite clearly as a 'bulge' in the testicles, between the hind legs. An umbilical hernia is visible at the centre of the belly, where the umbilical cord is attached; it can be as small as a pea, but is easily recognizable after the cord has dried up and dropped off. If you turn the piglet over on to his back and press the bulge gently, it will 'pop' back in, out of sight; however, it will reappear afterwards. Occasionally I have had piglets whose umbilical hernias have been very small and unidentifiable until the piglet has put on weight and his belly is quite round.

However small, hernias should not be dismissed – they are a hereditary problem, and animals displaying any sort of hernia should be eliminated from your breeding programme.

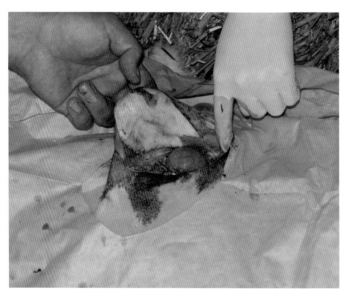

LEFT: *Umbilical hernia in a calf. (Courtesy Dominic Alexander MRCVS, Belmont Vets, Hereford)*

OPPOSITE TOP RIGHT: *The opening through which the hernia protrudes. (Courtesy Dominic Alexander MRCVS, Belmont Vets, Hereford)*

OPPOSITE BOTTOM RIGHT: *The hernia repaired and stitched. This operation is on a calf but exactly the same procedure would be used to operate on a pig. (Courtesy Dominic Alexander MRCVS, Belmont Vets, Hereford)*

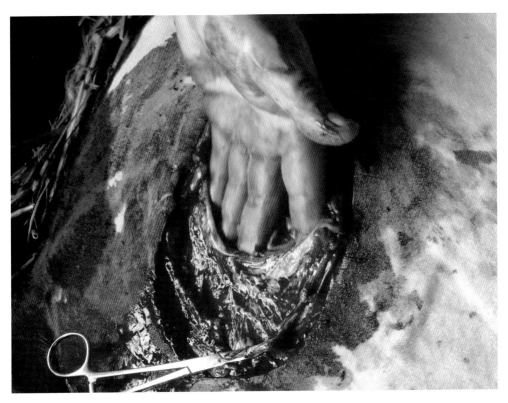

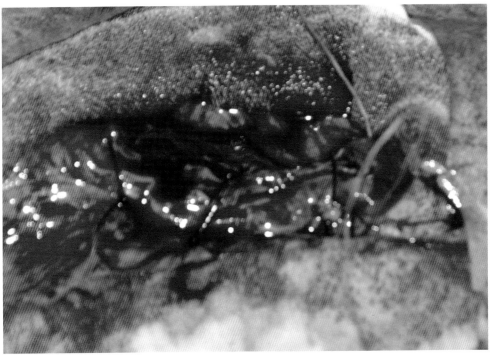

Treatment

The treatment of hernias is possible in many cases. It is expensive – about the value of the piglet itself if it is sold on as a castrate to be kept as a companion pig. However, if the piglet has a good permanent home to go to, I always think it is worth the money and the effort to give him a chance, as his quality of life should be as good as that of any other pig after the operation.

Testicular/inguinal/abdominal hernias can be repaired with an operation where a piece of 'mesh' is inserted into the abdomen. This mesh will repair the rupture in the tissue.

The operation itself is similar to that performed on a small animal such as a dog or cat. Your vet may or may not be willing to operate, and as with all operations, there is a significant risk of losing a pig under general anaesthetic.

Are Hernias Hereditary?

What is the hereditary nature of these defects? Since as early as the 1920s, researchers have been trying to establish the hereditary nature, if any, of these defects. There are reports that confirm genetic contribution to hernias. However, there is not sufficient information to confirm a simple Mendelian inheritance (the involvement of a few genes) for these disorders.

Dr Patrick K. Charagu, 2005

Cleft Palate

Cleft palate is a problem in the soft palate in the roof of the mouth. The palate is not fully formed, and in some cases the piglet will not be able to suckle at all and will die quite soon after birth. If you put your fingers into the roof of the piglet's mouth, a deep cavity can be felt.

Symptoms: A lack of growth and normal development is the most obvious symptom of a pig with a cleft palate. You may also hear coughing or choking noises at feeding time, because the piglet will take milk into the respiratory tract when suckling – milk may appear out of the snout at the same time.

Treatment

As with hernias, it is possible to operate successfully on a piglet with a cleft palate, although it is expensive and with the afore-mentioned associated risks. However, if these obstacles are overcome, the pig should go on to develop normally and lead a healthy life.

Cleft palate is a congenital defect and pigs exhibiting this problem should be eliminated from your breeding programme.

Joint Ill

Joint ill is an infection in the joints generally contracted through poor hygiene in the farrowing house. It is caused by bacteria entering the system through the umbilical cord at birth. It can manifest itself at any time from pre-weaning age up to several months old.

Symptoms: Lameness, hot painful swelling of the joints, possible fever and unwillingness to leave the nest, or frequent lying down to rest.

Treatment

Joint ill can be treated with a course of penicillin, but in severe cases can leave lasting damage to the joints. Prevention is far better than cure, and good hygiene, spraying of the umbilical cord shortly after birth, and care and cleanliness after the birth will prevent this condition.

Prolapse of the Rectum

Prolapse of the rectum can occur in piglets, although it is uncommon in outdoor herds. Overcrowding or cold farrowing quarters can be a contributory factor as piglets huddling together for warmth may be more susceptible due to the pressure on the abdomen. Tail docking is another possible cause, as damage to the nerve endings can cause relaxation of the sphincter muscle.

Symptoms: Constipation, the appearance of red tissue from the anus, blood in the faeces.

Treatment
There is no suitable treatment and the piglet should be humanely destroyed.

Prolapse is not thought to be hereditary.

Pneumonia

Pneumonia is fairly common in piglets. It can be caused by damp conditions, draughts or constant changes in temperature, as well as birth fluid or milk in the lung. Pneumonia also occurs in adult pigs and weaners.

Symptoms: Rapid breathing, coughing and loss of appetite. Older pigs will show fewer symptoms and may just appear 'off colour'. In this case I would always suspect the chest to be the problem and treat accordingly. If pneumonia progresses, the pig will run a temperature.

Treatment
Treatment with antibiotics and anti-inflamma-

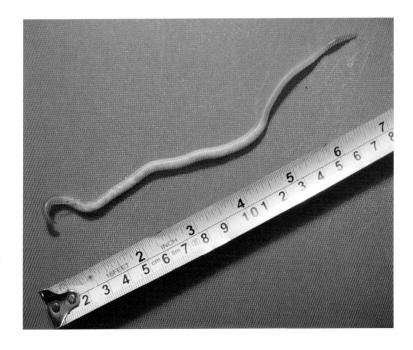

Worming is a vital part of animal husbandry. Worms like this one will quickly multiply and cause untold damage if not eradicated.

Piglet suffering from mange. The skin on his belly is dry and reddening and beginning to look sore.

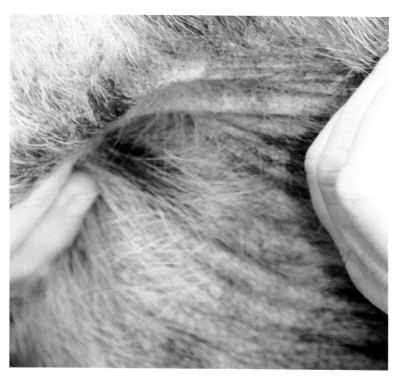

Thick scabs have started to form on his forelegs, and his chest is also dry and sore.

tories is essential, and the earlier treatment is given, the more likely it is to be successful. If pneumonia is severe it can leave scarring on the lungs, which will affect the long term health of the pig. Pneumonia can be fatal in pigs of any age.

Worms and Parasites

Worms and skin parasites will really take their toll on pigs of all ages, so it is important to keep up a regular worming programme, and to keep good records of when pigs were wormed and what was used. Always pass this information on if you sell a pig so that the new owner can continue with worming at the correct time. Piglets will often develop mange – an external parasite – at weaning as a result of stress. Lice are common in pigs and although they do not create the same obvious soreness of the skin, they are detrimental to the overall health of the pig.

Symptoms:
Worms: Loss of condition, dry coat, swollen belly. Worms can sometimes be seen in the faeces.
Mange: Dry, sore or cracked skin, itching, loss of condition. Open sores will develop behind the ears, at the base of the tail and along the spine.
Lice: Itching and rubbing. Lice are clearly visible on a pig. Their eggs are bright yellow and about the size of a pin head, and will stick on to the hair; they will be easy to spot on the neck, around the base of the tail and in the creases at the top of the hind legs under the ham muscle.

Treatment
Treatment for internal parasites can be done with an oral wormer such as Flubenol (*see* Useful Addresses). An Ivermectin-based injection will treat internal and external parasites.

Scours

Scouring in piglets is fairly common. It may be superficial and will right itself within twenty-four hours. There are various causes of scouring, although it is mainly due to one of three common bacteria: E. coli, coccidiosis and salmonella.

A warm and very clean piglet area will help to prevent the problem. This means daily removal of any damp bedding; a clean, dry floor in the farrowing area; daily removal of all muck; and an absorbent floor covering such as wood shavings in the toilet area. Make sure your farrowing area is free from draughts, as chilling is another factor in the onset of scours. If scouring is severe or lasts for more than twenty-four hours it needs to be treated; if left untreated it can be fatal.

Symptoms: Loose or runny faeces, yellow, brown or green in colour.

Treatment
Antibiotic, given orally or injected. It is extremely important to make sure the piglets are drinking plenty of clean water. Dehydration is a secondary problem of scouring and can be fatal. In extreme scouring, a rehydration fluid of glucose and salt may be necessary.

PROBLEMS IN THE SOW

All sows will behave differently following the birth of a litter, but as a general rule I would expect a sow to be on her feet and hungry within twelve hours of the birth. I would expect her to urinate and defecate within this time, and in good weather to be up and outside foraging within twenty-four hours.

Her vulva should be clean and dry within hours of the birth, with no discharge or smell.

If a sow does not follow this pattern, I would take her temperature (38.6°C/102°F is normal) and get her checked over by a vet. Remember – you could accept with regret the loss of a piglet, but the loss of your sow could also mean the loss of your whole litter.

Be vigilant, and if in any doubt at all of her wellbeing, seek help. Most problems if treated early are not insurmountable, but if left to fester, time could mean the difference between life and death.

Mastitis

Mastitis is a common condition that occurs sporadically in individual sows. It starts around farrowing and becomes evident up to twelve hours later. It can arise because bacteria have gained entry to one or more mammary glands, or it may be a flare-up of a latent infection. The route of entry of the bacteria can be the teat orifice or from the bloodstream, or by injection on piglets' teeth. Mastitis can also occur when there is over-plentiful milk production.

Symptoms: You may first notice that piglets are restless, squealing and hungry. The sow may be aggressive towards them and refuse to feed them; in extreme cases she may attack and kill them. On examination the udder will feel hot and hard in places. If left untreated the sow will become ill and will run a temperature. Mastitis seems quite common in outdoor pigs as they come into contact with so many more bacteria than indoor pigs.

Treatment
Treatment with antibiotics is usually effective, but care must be taken to act early in order that the milk supply doesn't dry up. Mastitis can occur at farrowing time, just after farrowing and also at weaning time. After weaning check the sow every twelve hours for the first thirty-six hours. If she is bursting with milk and the udder is hard to the touch, let her back in with her piglets for a few minutes, but remove her again as soon as she has fed them. The next time you check the problem should have gone, but if it persists you will need to treat her as above.

Prolapse of the Rectum

Prolapse of the rectum can occur in sows or piglets. Generally found in housed rather than outdoor sows, rectal prolapse is caused by excessive pressure on the abdomen. This can be due to a number of things: an overweight sow carrying a large litter, constipation (usually caused by a low fibre diet), and overcrowded housing conditions in indoor units.

Symptoms: Prolapse of the rectum can be recognized by the relaxed sphincter muscle, showing a small red protrusion from the rectum. This will increase in size when the sow lies down. There will be bleeding or blood in the faeces. In indoor units this condition can give rise to cannibalism.

Treatment
This condition should correct itself after the sow has farrowed, and with correct management of the diet.

Prolapse of the Vagina and Cervix

An overweight sow in pig carrying a large litter will be more likely to suffer from this condition. It is caused by pressure on the cervix, and will be exacerbated by large piglets, constipation, and overcrowding of sleeping quarters. As farrowing approaches the condition may worsen.

Symptoms: A red protrusion from the vulva, particularly when the sow is lying down. This should disappear when she stands up, although it may not. She may strain as if constipated.

Treatment
Separate any sow that is suffering from this condition from other sows so she has room to lie comfortably in her bed without being squashed or crowded. If the protrusion does not disappear inside when the sow is standing, tape may be stuck across the vulva to aid its support. Unless very severe, this condition should correct itself when the sow farrows.

Prolapse of the Uterus

Prolapse of the uterus is fortunately an uncommon occurrence. Like the above, it is most likely in older, overweight sows carrying large litters, and those who have flaccid muscle tone of the uterus. Excessive straining during the birth can bring on a prolapse of the uterus.

Symptoms: Shortly after farrowing (usually from two to twelve hours) the red tissue of the uterus will start to bulge from the vaginal opening, followed by the emergence of the uterus in its entirety. Prior to prolapse, straining will be apparent, although in a farrowing sow this will not be distinguishable from normal contractions.

Treatment
Replacement of the uterus of a sow is possible, although it is a difficult and often unsuccessful process. The uterus itself will most likely be damaged, and the risk of infection will be very high. The sow will be distressed and in extreme pain, so the best course of treatment for this condition will be to humanely destroy her as soon as possible.

Thin Sow Syndrome

Thin sow syndrome is a gradual deterioration in condition over two or more breeding cycles, and can affect any sow. Affected sows are unable to convert food efficiently, and as a result will become emaciated.

Symptoms: Loss of condition, worsening with each subsequent litter. Eventual infertility, and failure to come into season. Cystitis and abortion can also indicate this condition.

Treatment
Affected sows should be kept in warm conditions with plenty of deep bedding, and fed ad lib on good quality feed. Their body condition score should be good before they are put to the boar again. During lactation they will need to be very well fed.

Agalactia (Lack of Milk)

Sometimes a sow will fail to produce milk when she farrows. The reasons for this can be stress during the birth, premature birth of a litter, poor condition of the sow, post partum infection, or simply failure to 'let down' the milk. Agalactia can follow an occurrence of mastitis.

Symptoms: Lack of milk coming through the udder. You may first notice this if the new piglets are restless, fighting, squealing and generally unsettled. There may be no fever present in the sow and the udder may appear full.

Treatment

A hormone injection will sometimes bring on the production of milk; following a stressful birth this, coupled with rest, may be all that is needed. If the sow has contracted an infection, successful treatment of the infection with antibiotics should remedy the situation. However, piglets may need milk substitute in the meantime.

Rejecting the Litter

The maternal instinct in most animals is strong and a pig is no exception. If your sow shows signs of rejecting her litter, there will undoubtedly be an underlying reason for this.

Symptoms: Restless behaviour from the sow, ranging from getting up and down frequently and turning around in the nest to obvious aggression and anxiety towards the piglets. Unhappy, cold, listless or squealing piglets, dead piglets.

Treatment

Establishing the cause of rejection is the key factor; in my own experience it is usually mastitis that causes a sow to reject her litter. The painful swelling of the udder forces her to go against all her natural instincts to feed and nurture her piglets, and leaves her bewildered and distressed as she cannot do this due to the sheer agony of trying to feed with an inflamed udder.

Mastitis is treatable, as discussed above, but it may be necessary for your vet to tranquillize the sow in order that you can leave the piglets with her. Failing this, you will need to remove the piglets from the sow until the infection is under control.

Other causes of litter rejection can be:

- stress – ensure that your sow has peace and quiet, and that she can farrow in an area which is familiar to her
- interference from outside – other pigs must be removed from the farrowing area and handling of newborn piglets kept to an absolute minimum
- inexperience – sometimes a maiden gilt will reject her litter simply through bewilderment at what is happening. She can be mildly sedated until her maternal instinct surfaces and she feels the need to feed the litter. A vet will need to be called to administer a sedative such as Stresnil, which should calm her down.

Afterbirth Retention

Retained afterbirth will cause metritis (inflammation of the uterus) in the sow, which in turn may lead to infection.

Symptoms: The sow will seem unthrifty, with a loss of appetite following the birth. She may show a brownish, possibly smelly discharge from the vagina, will develop a high temperature, and will possibly not produce milk. Other symptoms are vomiting, lack of balance and shivering.

Treatment

Veterinary treatment will be necessary, and antibiotics, possibly over a course of several days, until the infection is completely cleared.

Rupture to the Uterus

It is possible that the uterus will be torn during delivery. This can be caused by different factors: piglets getting stuck, trotters piercing the lining of the birth canal, or an internal examination.

Symptoms: Similar to those of retained after-birth, as infection will set in. An unthrifty sow, loss of appetite, high temperature, unwillingness to be up and active. Vomiting, loss of balance and cessation of milk production. Excessive blood loss during the birth may also indicate this problem, and blood loss following the birth.

Treatment
Treatment is unlikely to be successful, although a course of antibiotics can be tried. Ruptures may heal, depending on their severity and the severity of the consequential infection. If the sow does recover, she may lose the ability to breed again.

Infertility

If you have bred successfully from your sow and have had none of the above uterine problems, there is no reason at all why she should not continue to breed. Follow the guidelines set out in the chapter 'Hogging and Mating' on timing and sow condition scoring to keep her in the best of health and optimum breeding condition. As she ages, take care not to leave her too long between litters – a maximum of six months – and not to let her become overweight.

Symptoms: Failure to conceive a litter.

Treatment
Hormone injections. The success of treatment depends upon the cause of the infertility.

CHAPTER 10

MARKETING AND SELLING YOUR PIGLETS

If you are only breeding one litter of piglets for fun, you will most likely have no trouble selling them, possibly by word of mouth or without even advertising them. If you want to breed on a regular basis and sell several litters a year, then you will need to think about how, and for what, you will sell your piglets. Consider the space you have and whether you will want to grow some of them on to sell later, or to take to the abattoir for your own use.

Take time to consider again the commitment of breeding animals to sell: the piglets you produce are your responsibility, and even if their eventual destination is a slaughterhouse, ensure that you do everything you can to make their journey from birth to death, however short or long, a good one. Wherever you decide your market is to be, if you are selling live pigs on to new homes, always be sure to include in the sale a 'new owner pack'. This should contain the following information for the purchaser:

- Information specific to the pigs they are purchasing, including dates of birth, parent bloodlines, dates of worming and vaccinations, and dates when the next worming and vaccinations are due
- In the case of expectant mothers, the dates of service and expected dates of farrowing, and the details of the boar that served them
- Feed requirements and quantities to be fed
- Ear tag numbers
- General care information
- Breed information
- Helpline number for any problems arising

BREEDING STOCK

If you are interested in breeding your pigs to produce breeding stock, you will need to look into bloodlines, conformation, temperament and pedigrees in the very early stages of your venture. Be sure to set yourself up with the best breeding stock you can find. When you come to sell your weaners there will be plenty of others available out there, so your own will need to compare well with the competition.

Breeding to produce high standards of stock is very much a game of trial and error. For every good pig you produce, there will probably be ten that are not very good at all. Learning to recognize the good ones is tricky too, and only comes with experience. Many is the time that I have had a gilt of my own breeding come back to stud and I have secretly chastised myself for ever letting her go! The same can be said of stock I have thought would make super pigs, but which in the end have turned out to be mediocre. However, all is not lost because if the breeding behind them is good and sound, they will hopefully throw some good progeny.

If you intend trying to produce good breeding stock from your pigs your best market place will be the show ring. There are many shows that hold classes for pigs, from local agricultural shows to the big county shows. Look out for the show dates well in advance – they can be found on the internet or in good smallholding magazines (*see* Useful Addresses). Once you have marked on your calendar which shows you will be attending, you can plan your breeding accordingly: some sows will be in pig, some may be lactating and can be shown with the litter, and other youngstock can be shown individually.

The audience that you and your pigs will get if you exhibit is huge. Apart from the classes themselves, your pigs will be on display in the pig lines for anything up to five days, depending on the size of the show and the regulations regarding arrival and departure. You will be able to take along as much publicity material as you like in the way of display boards, breed information and your own promotional leaflets, and you can hand these out to prospective purchasers.

Apart from showing off your stock, there is also the benefit of networking at shows. You will get a chance to meet other breeders, look at and learn from their stock, buy, sell and exchange stock with other breeders, and, most importantly, make good contacts for the future. You will also learn a lot about your own pigs when you can see them in comparison with others: a breed standard is all very well but is not worth the paper it's written on if you never see a true example of it in the flesh.

When you actually get into the show ring, if you are not lucky enough to win a prize, you

Pig lines at shows are an excellent advertisement for your stock; you can also display information about your breed and any prizes you have won on the day.

Checklist for Pig Shows

- Movement licence (plus one for the return journey)
- All pigs ear tagged
- Feed and water containers
- Feed
- Water carrier/bucket
- Grooming equipment
- Shampoo
- Board and stick
- Overalls for working in pig lines
- Wellingtons or waterproof footwear that can be disinfected
- Clean white coat for the show ring
- Shirt and tie
- Clean footwear for the show ring
- String
- Safety pins for attaching your show numbers
- Staple gun (for pinning up those rosettes!)
- Publicity material/business cards/leaflets
- Emergency vet kit (wound powder/ wound spray, mild disinfectant, cotton wool, thermo-meter, vinegar)
- Pig oil
- Tools for cleaning out pig pens
- Broom, for keeping your area of the pig lines clean and tidy

---

will learn more about your own animals from comparing them to others that do win, and from talking to the judge and other exhibitors, than you ever knew before. Most judges will be happy to talk about the decisions they have made and explain their preferences. If you are amongst the prize winners, you will be able to display your winnings on your pig pens and potentially improve the value of your stock. If you do well with a pig that is not your own breeding, he or she is still a credit to you and will be producing good offspring for you to sell.

Whatever the outcome of a visit to a show, you will have begun to build yourself a market. Showing is not for everyone, but if you are serious about producing good stock and building a good reputation as a breeder, then it is important to get yourself and your pigs out there and get them noticed.

If you really can't face the show ring for whatever reason, you could always exhibit your pigs at countryside shows on a breed society stand or just as an attraction for visitors. Many small shows will welcome the opportunity to have you along with a few well behaved and friendly pigs for people to admire. Again you can take your own publicity material and information about the breed and hand these things out to interested parties. You will be surprised how far those leaflets will travel even after the show is over.

A final word of advice on exhibiting pigs or piglets at shows: I personally never sell pigs from a showground except to people I know or have already had contact with in some way regarding the sale of pigs.

Shows are lovely places to learn about and visit livestock, and sometimes we get caught up in the 'thrill' of the day. Impulse buys of hats, boots or fancy garden ornaments are one thing, but buying livestock is something which needs careful consideration. Don't sell your stock to impulse buyers who may regret their decision the next day. If folk seem genuinely interested, give them your contact details and wait for them to come back to you after the show. A percentage of them most certainly will, but those who are not seriously interested in keeping pigs won't.

All showgrounds, large or small, are of course subject to the usual Defra rules and regulations, and at the larger shows there will be Animal Health and Trading Standards officials present to ensure the rules are followed. Smaller showgrounds will not have such tight restrictions, but you will need to check with them first that they have a county parish holding (CPH) number on the land they are using for the show. If they don't have this, you will need to get permission from your local trading standards office to take your pigs on and off the showground.

Larger shows will also have strict entry and exit times for pigs so you may have to be prepared for several days stay on the showground. Your transport will also need to be in line with Welfare in Transit (WIT) laws, and of course, cleaned and disinfected prior to the journey.

Remember that all pigs travelling to a show will need to be ear tagged regardless of age –

and don't forget to fill in your movement licence.

EXPORTING PIGS

When you are confident of the standard of stock you are producing, another outlet you could investigate is the export market. Exporting within the European Union is actually classed as 'intra community trade' and is considerably easier than exporting further afield. Each individual member state has its own requirements, and you will need to familiarize yourself with these in the first instance either by contacting Defra, who will send you the information, or by looking on the Defra website (*see* Useful Addresses) where you will find these requirements listed.

Isolation, blood testing (in some cases) and transport are areas you will need to look into, and be sure you are suitably equipped and/or licensed for each one. Transport regulations can be obtained from the Welfare of Animals in Transit (WIT) office (*see* Useful Addresses). In all cases a veterinary health certificate will be required, and as the exporter, you will need to apply for this several weeks in advance of the intended departure date of the pigs.

All pigs travelling abroad must have their ear-tag identification number prefixed with the letter 'P'.

Once these initial provisions have been made you will be able to spread your wings a little further and send your breeding stock and your reputation further afield!

If you do have enquiries from abroad, check out all the costs and any quarantine requirements which you can forward to your customer before they make their final decision; importing pigs can be expensive, so be sure to set out the costs and arrange for a deposit before making transport bookings or holding piglets for overseas customers.

Checklist for Exporting Pigs

▨ Check out ports of departure and arrival for specific requirements
▨ Check veterinary requirements for the destination country
▨ Check ferry company requirements for pigs
▨ Book blood testing (if necessary) approximately four weeks in advance of the departure date
▨ Ear tag pigs for travel
▨ Apply to Defra exports office for veterinary health certificate for the export of pigs
▨ Complete journey log (where applicable)
▨ Book ferry crossings
▨ Book veterinary health check for within twenty-four hours of departure

Once blood tests have been done, pigs must depart within thirty days. Once your health certificate has been issued, you must complete your journey within ten days.

If you intend to transport the pigs yourself, you will need to provide a journey log for the Defra export office. This document sets out your intended route, mode of transport, specifics of the pigs, timings and any rest stops you intend to make. The journey log will be approved by the Welfare of Animals in Transit office when your veterinary export health certificate is issued.

In some cases the customer may be willing to collect the piglets from you, which will make the export considerably easier than if you have to deliver.

PIGS FOR FINISHING

Should you decide to sell your weaners on for 'finishing' you should not have much difficulty finding good buyers who can provide your pigs with a suitable environment to live in. There are many families and individuals nowadays who choose to rear their own meat: those who have a conscience about where their meat comes from and how it has

been produced, and are fortunate enough to have the space, are more than happy to do this.

Weaners being sold on for fattening will need to be wormed and in excellent condition, and accompanied by the above-mentioned new owners' pack containing the relevant information.

Meat: For You or To Sell

Growing on your own weaners for fattening and finishing is a subject covered in many pig books specializing in producing pigs for the table. Nevertheless, the need for forward planning should again be stressed, because unless you are intending to sell on your meat in farmers' markets or at food festivals, through local outlets or to the restaurant trade, you should keep your breeding to sensible numbers. Stagger your litters so that your animals will be ready at different stages, and then you will not have a glut of meat – unless of course you have huge freezers!

If your meat is purely for your own consumption you may consider having a home kill in order to reduce the stress on your pigs and yourselves, and to avoid having to acquire the correct transport in order to take your pigs to slaughter at an abattoir. However, if your pigs are killed at home, at the time of writing it is against the law to sell the meat because all meat sold for human consumption must be slaughtered at an abattoir and inspected to be sure that it meets specified standards.

The meat you receive back from your butcher will be packaged according to your requirements, and you may then sell it as and when you wish, and through whichever outlets you may choose.

If selling your meat in this manner, you may choose to market it through your own website or through farmers' market-type forums on the internet. You can also research prices this way, and make sure you are selling your meat competitively after taking into account the expenses you have incurred in order to produce it.

SELLING TO FARMS/ AGRICULTURAL COLLEGES/ AS PETS

If selling your stock to open farms, children's farms, travelling farms or even colleges, the pigs will need to be very friendly and well socialized. All pigs, no matter what breed, are open to socialization; pigs on the whole are intelligent creatures which delight in human company, and a little time spent with them post-weaning, every day until they leave home, will be time well spent.

If you have a particularly nervous or stand-offish litter, once the worming injections, ear tagging and any other unpleasant jobs are done, keep them in a confined space, possi-

bly a livestock trailer or a stable, and take some time to sit with them each day. Offer them delicious treats such as apple pieces or banana, and let them come to you. They will soon decide that you are good company and not to be feared.

Outlets such as open farms are ideal: they can offer excellent facilities for keeping pigs, and if they are happy with the stock they have bought from you they will usually be agreeable to putting up a small advertisement for you such as 'pigs supplied by…', which will be seen by hundreds of people if the venue is open to the public or hosts public events – an excellent form of free advertising.

Selling pigs as pets is a controversial subject at the time of writing. With the current explosion in the UK of 'micro pigs' – a cross-breed of pig that has so far proved to be something of a disaster – the general pet pig-buying public has quite rightly lost faith. Many of these pigs have outgrown their 'micro' status before reaching twelve months of age – only half way towards their eventual growth expectancy – and many have found their way into unsuitable environments.

Selling pigs as pets is a big responsibility. Many people who are seduced into the idea of pet pigs by cute pictures of piglets in teacups and baskets are blissfully unaware of the long-term commitment and the possible difficulties they will be taking on. If considering selling your pigs as pets, be sure to sell them only to customers who can offer a long-term home with the correct facilities for pigs – at least half an acre of grazing-rooting ground, warm winter housing (not inside the owners' house!), and shade and a wallow for the summer months. There are many considerations when selling pigs as pets: here are just a few to remind your potential buyers of what they are taking on:

- Pet pigs are subject to the same legal requirements and documentation as farm pigs, including identification, movement licences, medical record keeping and isolation
- Always sell pigs in groups of two or more, unless the buyer already has porcine company for the pig. A dog or cat or other domestic pet will not do as company for a pig
- Pigs need correct transport in the event of a visit to the vet
- Someone will need to care for the pigs while you are away on holiday
- Uncastrated boars must not be sold as pets as they may become aggressive at sexual maturity
- A pig can make a noise which reaches the same level in decibels as a jet engine with its after-burners on! How will the neighbours feel about this?
- In the event of a notifiable disease outbreak in the UK, pet pigs will be slaughtered, just as farm pigs are slaughtered to prevent the spread of disease

Choose your buyers carefully. Your pigs are relying on you to ensure they have a long, happy and settled life.

ADVERTISING

When you are ready to advertise your pigs, decide who you think your most likely customers will be and then advertise in the appropriate place. Your advertising will of course depend on two major factors: your budget and your intended market.

Probably the most economical and efficient form of advertising these days is the internet. Websites can be built to suit any budget and can be easily maintained, even by an amateur computer user. You may be able simply to add a pig 'page' to an existing website, depending of course on the content of the site and its relevance to your pig breeding. If you intend 'building' a website specifically for your own pig production and sales you will need photographs, information and, most importantly, time to update it: there is nothing worse from the customer's point of view than finding a website which appears to have just what they are looking for and then finding it is completely out of date with its information.

Apart from having a website of your own, there are many opportunities to advertise on other people's websites. There are smallholder websites which advertise all manner of things, some free of charge and some at a price (*see* Useful Addresses). Again, keep your advertisements current – that alone will give you the edge over those advertisers who don't.

Another advertising outlet is in the press, and there are good smallholder magazines, farming and livestock magazines on the market with breeders' lists in the advertising pages, which work well. However, although breeder listings are very good value for money, they are only worthwhile if you have piglets for sale for several months of the year.

These days it really is essential to be 'computer literate' if you wish to promote your business to a wide market, and one way to do this is to get involved with message boards and forums (*see* Useful Addresses). There are pet, farming, lifestyle and smallholder forums, some of which have a huge network of pig keepers, potential customers and enthusiasts. These forums are not only useful for sales, but also for advice and support. Many experienced pig keepers are happy to offer help, which is invaluable and often there at hand when you need it most: in my own experience it has often been beneficial to use a forum when I needed to seek help in a crisis.

Advertisements in local papers, veterinary surgeries, feed merchants and agricultural suppliers can also be useful, particularly if you are selling weaners for finishing. I avoid advertising my pigs to the 'pet' market because pet websites and forums are aimed more at the householder than the smallholder in my opinion. Nevertheless this is a personal choice and one which you may research for yourself.

REPUTATION AND AFTERCARE

Whatever advertising medium you choose, remember that it's not just your pigs you are selling, but also yourself as a breeder: build yourself a good reputation and people will come back to you, send their friends to you and recommend you to others. This is a fact, but the reverse is even more significant in that if you upset your customers the news will travel like wildfire!

Whatever you are selling, whether piglets or washing machines, reputation and after sales service are more important to your customers than anything else. Therefore try to live by the old adage 'the customer is always right': this may not always be true, but in the long run it is well worth it to you to accept criticism, be gracious, and if your customer is not happy, to give them a replacement or a refund or whatever it is they seek. You may lose money on this occasion, but a happy customer in the hand is worth two in the bush! Your reputation will build itself, and word of mouth is the best form of advertising. Besides, think of the pigs: if the customer is not happy with them, doesn't want them, or for some other reason has to be rid of them, the pigs are the most likely to suffer in this scenario. Sort the problem out as easily and cost effectively as you can, and you will be able to sleep soundly in your bed at night.

Remember that a reputation is not developed overnight: it has to be earned slowly from your very first litter and your very first customer – but once it's there and built on firm ground, it will not be easily lost.

Aftercare is essential to the welfare of the pigs you are selling, particularly if your customers are new to pig keeping. Helping out costs nothing but will make a world of difference to the pig keeper who lacks knowledge, experience and confidence, and therefore to the pigs he is keeping.

PRICING

Many 'hobby' pig keepers will not take into account their time when working out their profits as they consider their time to be a commodity they can give away freely, and pig keeping to be a 'labour of love'. This is all well and good, but be sure to take into account all the other expenses you have incurred when setting a price on your pigs. It is, of course, entirely up to you what you charge for your piglets, but remember that if you don't value them, the chances are that other people won't either.

Price will vary tremendously depending on the breed of pig, the age, sex, breeding capability and of course the purpose for which the pig is being sold. Location will also play a part, in that if you are geographically central then you will probably have more success selling your stock than someone who lives at Land's End or John O'Groats! Selling in more affluent areas of the country may also have its bearing, although if you can deliver your pigs to their destination, geographical factors may be overcome.

If you are selling weaners for finishing,

your purchaser will be looking to grow them on and supply himself with meat cost effectively; if you are selling pigs as pets, the purchaser will hopefully be looking forward to many years of companionship and enjoyment. Often when I have quoted the going rate for a pet pig I have had the reply that they can 'go down to the market and get a piglet for a fiver'. My reply has to be 'Then go to the market and buy one – don't come to me'. The difference between the weaner you can buy at the market and the pet pig sold at several times the price is simple: the pet pig should be suitably bred to be exactly that, and the other is not. If I were looking for a gundog I wouldn't buy a Yorkshire Terrier: I would buy a Retriever.

If your customers are looking for a 'pet' or companion pig, try to persuade them to take a castrated boar. Castrates are the most docile, affectionate and companionable animals I have ever come across. Gilts may become hormonal at breeding age, and two gilts together which are not breeding can be-come snappy with each other. Your castrates may be 'only pigs' but they are invaluable for the job they are bred to do. It's also a good idea to have a considerable price difference between gilts and castrated boars, to encourage people to buy the boys if they don't need breeding potential. There will always be a healthy market for breeding gilts, even when they are a little older, but purchasers looking for pet pigs will usually want to buy while the piglets are still young.

Rare breed pigs will command higher prices than other breeds, particularly if they are good examples of the breed. Breeding stock and certainly more sought-after bloodlines may raise the price even more.

The age of your pigs for sale is also important, so be fair with your prices – thus a proven boar pig in his prime has to be worth more than a boar piglet who has not yet proved himself and requires bringing on and feeding up for the next twelve months before the purchaser will see any return on his outlay. And a sow in pig can potentially

---

Expenses and Pricing

The following checklist itemizes the expenses that should be taken into account when pricing your pigs:

- Feed
- Bedding
- Maintenance costs, such as worming, vaccinations
- Veterinary costs
- Transportation costs
- Stud costs
- Labour
- Castrations
- Ear tags/tattoos/slap markers
- General maintenance and repairs, such as housing, fencing

produce ten beautiful piglets for your purchaser, but then again, she may only produce two!

If you really are not sure what to charge, phone around some other breeders and find out what the going rate is so you can pitch your prices alongside the rest of the market. However, do not be tempted to undercut the competition – if you do this the end result will be a devaluation of the product that you are trying to sell.

Finally, when you sell your stock, give some goodwill with the sale: thus assure the purchaser that if there are immediate problems, you will honour your commitment by replacing/refunding or simply helping to put the problem right for him. In short, 'do unto others as you would have them do to you'. Good customers will pay a fair price for something that they think worth having.

FREQUENTLY ASKED QUESTIONS

Q. What age should my gilt be before I start to breed from her?

A. Between twelve and eighteen months.

Q. How do I know which bloodlines to use?

A. Check your pig's pedigree and do not use a bloodline that appears in the first generation.

Q. How can I tell when my gilt is in season?

A. Signs will be a swollen vulva, standing still with her tail twitching, and noisiness. With a boar present this should be easy as she will not move far from where the boar is.

Q. How will I know for sure that my sow is pregnant?

A. She will not come back into season after the mating has taken place. Further signs will become evident in the last four weeks of her gestation, including enlarged teats, swelling of the belly, and enlarged vulva.

Q. What should I feed my pregnant sow?

A. Throughout the pregnancy don't change your usual feeding programme. Increase the feed steadily after farrowing.

Q. Should I keep a boar back for breeding?

A. No, not unless you are experienced and really know what to look for in a boar, and even then I would only keep a boar back if you have a definite buyer for him.

Q. At what age should I castrate my boar piglets?

A. Between two and four weeks. Consult your vet well in advance.

Q. How will I know when my sow is going to farrow?

A. Her vulva will become very swollen and slack, milk may come from the teats, she will appear very uncomfortable, and will begin to nest. She may also go off her food and produce a quantity of small, soft droppings.

Q. When should I separate my sow from her companions?

A. There is really no need to separate her until she is almost ready to have her piglets. About one week before farrowing try to settle her into her new quarters.

Q. Will my boar be able to stay with my sow when she farrows?

A. No. You are more likely to lose piglets if there are two bodies in the nest as they will get squashed. The boar would also mate with the sow as soon as she returned in season, possibly within a couple of weeks of her giving birth, which is not a good idea.

Q. How much should I feed my sow when she has had her piglets?

A. Gradually increase her feed from the second day, so that by the time the piglets are three weeks old she is eating 3–6lb for herself (depending on breed) and ½lb for every piglet she is feeding. (Use at least a 16 per cent protein pig food.)

Q. At what age will the piglets start to eat solid food?

A. They will start to steal a little from their mother at about two weeks. There is no need to feed extra to piglets while they are drinking from their mother.

Q. When should I wean my piglets?

A. When they are six to eight weeks old, depending on the size of the litter. If there are more than eight piglets it may drag the mother down to leave them on her for too long and she will become very thin and poor.

Q. What should I feed my weaners?

A. Approximately 1lb each for every month of their life: thus at three months old give 3lb of feed per day, divided into two feeds. Exceptions are Kunekune and Pot-Bellied weaners, where 1lb of feed per piglet per day will suffice from weaning to adulthood. Never feed more than 16 per cent protein to Kunekune and Pot Bellies, and 12 per cent is preferable.

Q. How do I register my piglets?

A. You will need to be a member of the BPA to register traditional breeds, and for Kunekunes, the British Kunekune Pig Society. You must litter notify your piglets by six weeks of age; they can then be registered to their new owners at a later date, up to twelve months of age. Forms are available from the secretary or on the appropriate websites.

Q. Should I hand feed the little one?

A. If you really think he is not getting enough to eat then you could feed him with extra sow milk replacer, but always leave him with his mum and siblings.

Q. Should I clip my piglets' teeth?

A. There is absolutely no need to clip teeth. A little face biting is normal whilst piglets are establishing themselves on a teat.

Q. Should I dock my piglets' tails?

A. No.

Q. Should I use a heat lamp on the piglets?

A. Using a heat lamp is a good idea even in warmer weather as it encourages the piglets to sleep away from the mother where they are less likely to be rolled on.

Q. My piglets are messing inside the arc and I thought pigs didn't do this. What should I do?

A. In very cold or wet weather even adult pigs will sometimes use the corner of the arc for a toilet. Young piglets will 'wet the bed' as they are sleeping but will always go to the edge of the sleeping area when they want to defecate. As they get older they will go further from the sleeping area and should naturally progress to the outdoors.

APPENDIX II

CASE STUDIES

What follows are a few true stories of pigs of mine which have had litters that for one reason or another stand out in my memory. Some are sad, some have a happy outcome, and some a little of both. Hopefully these will give you an idea of what can happen, what should happen, and what you really don't want to happen! Whatever the outcomes, I hope you enjoy reading them and find them helpful in some way.

CASE NO. 1: REABSORBING THE LITTER

Pod was a two-year-old gilt. She had shown all the normal signs of hogging and had conceived a litter at the first mating. Her gestation seemed very healthy and she had developed in every way I expected her to. I had seen the mating take place, and was absolutely sure of her expected date of delivery.

A few days before her EDD, Pod had developed a good milk bag and was now looking enormous – indeed, I had stood next to her and remarked that there was no ground clearance under her belly at all. I had gently stroked her belly with my foot and noticed that I couldn't slip my foot between her belly and the ground. I had felt healthy movements and quite distinctive kicking in the final week.

The due date came and went, which in itself was not unusual, but three days after she was due I noticed that there was a little ground clearance under her belly after all. I dismissed this, thinking that she must just be standing in a different position, and continued to wait for a litter.

The following day – four days late – I noticed a pink discharge coming from Pod's vagina. I took this to mean that she was in the early stages of labour, and duly became very excited. By the end of the day nothing had happened, and by the next day the pink discharge had turned from pink to red to brown and Pod was beginning to look a little unhappy and uncomfortable – so I asked the vet to come and have a look.

After a lengthy examination the vet was quite sure there were no piglets inside our pig. She was injected, and we waited to see what would happen. Later that day Pod went through what was a fairly normal farrowing, but the only thing to appear was one dead piglet, which from its condition had obviously been dead for some time. The rest of the litter, which had seemed healthy only days before, had been reabsorbed into her system.

Pod's recovery was slow. The infection left by the dead piglet took a hold and brought her down, and she lay hot and motionless in her bed for two days.

She pined for her unborn piglets, there was no doubt in my mind about that. When she did get up from her bed and began to make a recovery from the infection her grief was obvious: she became very vocal and paced the yard and paddock in what I interpreted as a pathetic 'hunt' for her offspring.

Sadly she never conceived again and died at the age of seven. A post mortem examination revealed large growths in her uterus.

CASE NO. 2: A NORMAL, HEALTHY FARROWING

Sybil was two years old to the day when her first litter was born. She was bagged up with milk and ready for the event, so I was keeping a close eye on her. The farrowing area was ready in the barn and Sybil was wandering sedately from field to yard to garden through the early morning. Then at breakfast time she had disappeared completely!

It didn't take me long to find her – a walk around the farm led me to the orchard where we were growing our hay so the grass was long and lush at the end of June. Sybil had flattened a huge area by shuffling in circles, and had ripped up mouthfuls of it to make a comfortable nest. Her nesting could have taken no more than half an hour, because when I came upon her she was already nursing two tiny ginger and black spotted piglets.

After equipping myself with all the essentials for a day's farrowing in a field – including camera, sunscreen (for Sybil, of course!) snacks and drinks (for me!) I settled down to watch Sybil give birth to eight more piglets. They arrived at regular intervals throughout the day, the whole process taking from approximately 9am to 4pm.

Sybil lay motionless throughout the birth, although she occasionally answered me when I spoke to her. We never left her un-guarded as we live in an area heavily populated with buzzards, and later on in the evening when Sybil seemed ready we put the whole litter into a washing basket, brought a bucket of apples to the orchard and Sybil followed both down the track and back to the barn where she was safely installed.

CASE NO. 3: A LENGTHY PROCESS

Ellie had a bad reputation when I bought her aged three years. She had had a couple of litters prior to my buying her, but had not proved to be the most sensible of mums, having once farrowed up against a door and every piglet had passed underneath the door into the night and perished, and the second time had chosen a ditch on a rainy evening, instead of her arc, which filled with water as she lay in labour and the whole litter drowned.

The night she decided to farrow was similarly a very stormy one, the rain coming down in steel rods as I lay in my warm bed watching the start of Ellie's nesting on the CCTV. Now and again she would disappear from view as she scoured the barn for nesting materials and occasionally relieved herself in the far corners. As her nesting intensified at around midnight she disappeared from view yet again – but never returned. After some time it became apparent that she really *had* disappeared from where she was meant to be, so I got dressed and went out.

The barn doors, which had been tied with rope, had been forced open from the inside – no mean feat in itself – and Ellie was nowhere to be found. Fortunately she is a very light cream pig and with the help of a torch she was eventually located at the bottom of the garden under some trees in the pouring rain. I hastily returned her to the barn where, following her long walk, she soon got under way with her farrowing.

It was a fairly long and slow operation – each time I thought she had finished another piglet would appear, and by morning, five were born and the afterbirth had appeared. Ellie was evidently 'done and dusted'. I was working shifts at this time and left for work at lunchtime, satisfied that she was none the worse for her ordeal and all five piglets were suckling and appeared healthy.

My shift ended at 6pm and I hurried home to see my new arrivals and to check that all was well. It was, but to my astonishment there were now seven piglets and more afterbirth: Ellie must have waited almost twelve hours between the two 'sides' of her uterus. For me she has always held the record of the longest farrowing – twenty-four hours! All the piglets survived and were healthy despite the long delay in the proceedings.

CASE NO. 4: THE SADDEST OF ALL

Sybil had always farrowed with no trouble and this, her final litter, was no exception: now six years old, she was an 'old hand' at the job and seven piglets were born after an apparently normal labour. Sybil, although tired and quiet, seemed none the worse for it.

The piglets were born in the evening, and it was well on into the night before the last one was delivered so I didn't bother to rouse her from her bed but left her to rest. But when I went out to check on her first thing in the morning it was obvious that she hadn't moved, as she was in the same position and the bedding was undisturbed. I tried to encourage her from her bed but she was not interested, even with the sound of her breakfast approaching. It was time to call the vet.

Sybil didn't have a temperature and there was no discharge apart from the obvious one that you would expect immediately after a farrowing.

Her udder was not troubling her, and there was no unpleasant smell which you might expect if an infection were setting in due to retained afterbirth or a dead piglet still in the womb. Everything appeared perfectly normal, but she was obviously troubled and in pain.

In the days that followed she completed two separate courses of antibiotics, complaining bitterly about the endless injections and only leaving her bed to relieve herself. She fed her piglets, but was only producing the bare minimum of milk – just enough to feed them, but no more, as her body could not apparently work any harder. Her appetite was almost non-existent and I was feeding her anything that she would eat – fruit, tinned rice pudding and tubs of cream – anything that took her fancy, as pig food didn't and something had to keep her alive and producing milk.

Then one afternoon when I looked out of the kitchen window she was in the garden. My heart leapt in relief, and I thought she must be on the mend. The piglets were two weeks old, and this was the first time she had been outside, I assumed to graze. It had been a long road to this little spark of recovery, and I had had many sleepless nights trying to work out what was wrong and hoping that it would right itself. Sybil was my first breeding sow and will always be the one closest to my heart: she taught me a lot about pigs and farrowing, and gave me endless hours of joy and amusement.

Then on 26 February when her piglets were three weeks old she had a massive fit and died.

She had not been outside again after I saw her that afternoon in the garden – almost as though she were having one last look around her old territory. Since that time her meals had become fewer and smaller, and the last one I remember was the morning she died: a bowl of porridge with honey on it, which I fed her with a spoon as she lay in bed.

At tea time I checked her and her breathing was fast and short. I took her temperature and it was up. I rang the vet and although he was out on a call he rang me back within a few minutes. As I took the call I was watching Sybil on CCTV from the kitchen. As I described her condition to the vet yet again, I saw her get up from her bed, stagger drunkenly across the floor and begin to shake violently. I ran from the house, as my first thought was that she would tumble on to the piglets and hurt them. But I shouldn't have worried – Sybil had known that she needed to get away from them, and had staggered across the pen where she shook and trembled violently: then she dropped to the ground and died.

We never knew for sure what the cause of her death really was, and I'm quite sure that even if we had known, it would not have been possible to save her. The official cause of death was a ruptured uterus.

I have had a lot of different thoughts about that awful time over the years, and although some of them may have been fuelled by my emotion and my attachment to Sybil, the one thing that I am sure of is that she struggled on for as long as was possible in order to raise her piglets to a point where they could survive without her. At three weeks of age, they were theoretically capable of survival without her milk.

I reared the litter on, but sadly lost two – the piglets were small and weak when Sybil died, and had had a poor start. But I still have her daughter, and she breeds regularly and is a fine sow.

CASE NO. 5: THE LONER

Sherry was a six-year-old sow, in quite good condition, and I acquired her because I had bought her daughter and mum was thrown in with the deal! But looking at the daughter, it was obvious that Sherry produced good stock, so I duly put her in pig.

Four months later I eagerly awaited the litter: Sherry was not particularly bothered by my presence although she didn't know me well, so I settled down in the barn to watch her farrow. She was bang on time with her due date and her nesting and preparations had seemed normal – two or three hours and we were well on the way.

But as the piglets appeared my heart sank lower and lower into my boots: one after another they arrived, but all dead and hideously deformed – some absolutely tiny, perhaps 4in in length, and some the size of normal piglets; some were badly decomposed, and some looked as though they should be alive, but weren't. Six poor little misshapen bodies, some with only two legs, some with no eyes, and some with no hair appeared before Sherry finally gave up the struggle and relaxed her old body into sleep.

I cleared up the mess and collected up the piglets for disposal, filled her water and left her lamp on to make her feel comfortable. As I left the barn I glanced at her beautiful swollen udder which would never be put to use, and felt a huge regret.

An hour later I looked in on Sherry to check that she had cleansed – and lo and behold, a perfect little ginger and black boar piglet was suckling away at the udder! Probably all the dead piglets were in one side of Sherry's uterus, and for some reason they had died at different stages of development, which was why some were badly decomposed and some not. Why they were not aborted or reabsorbed

'The loner' and his mum. He grew into a healthy little pig and now lives in Shropshire where he continues to thrive.

sooner, I don't know. Just as amazing was that the little chap from the other side was unaffected by whatever had killed them, and was born hale and healthy.

Sherry was treated with a heavy dose of antibiotics and was fine, but I never bred from her again.

CASE NO. 6: PROLAPSE OF A YOUNG SOW

Treacle was a beautiful black sow that I could fortunately give a home to when her owners were no longer able to keep her. She was two years old and expecting her second litter: a lovely healthy sow that had had no trouble farrowing the first time, I was not expecting any problems and was looking forward to the birth. She was in excellent condition just before farrowing, and settled down one evening at about 5pm in her carefully built nest.

She produced eight lovely piglets in about four hours, and everything seemed fine; however I was not sure that she had finished as she was still straining quite hard. I phoned the vet and he, too, thought that maybe she had a last piglet to come; he advised me to feel inside to check if there were a piglet stuck, and then to give her a shot of oxytocin to help her close down. On examination there was no evidence of any other piglet, and following the oxytocin injection Treacle expelled her afterbirth and settled down.

I stayed with her for some time and was happy that she was no longer straining, and that she had cleansed and was comfortable – although I did observe that her vulva seemed quite slack still, and almost hanging open. At half past midnight I was satisfied there was no more to do, and left Treacle and a healthy litter of suckling piglets.

At 6am the following morning I sneaked into the barn in my pyjamas to make sure that all was well – and was greeted by a sight I hope I shall never see again: Treacle had prolapsed her uterus and was obviously very distressed. I got her back to her bed and tried to make her comfortable, and called the vet immediately; whilst we waited I sat with Treacle and made sure all the piglets stayed close to her so she would not feel the need to get up again.

Treacle was euthanased as soon as the vet arrived, lying in her nest with the piglets suckling. All eight piglets were reared by hand and survived, and I kept a gilt, Bunty, to replace her mother. Bunty has bred several litters now and has won best of breed, champion sow, and sow and litter classes.

BREEDS OF PIG

THE KUNEKUNE

Breed History

The Kunekune was a breed prized by the Maori race in New Zealand, who kept them and allowed them to live freely on their settlements. They were disinclined to roam far and were easy to fatten – 'Kunekune' means 'round and fat' in Maori.

Every part of the pig would be used when it was slaughtered, including its abundance of lard, which was invaluable for preserving other foods: these could be 'vacuum packed' in the lard for up to a couple of years.

Sadly with the introduction of Western diets, pre-packed and preserved food, the breed became almost extinct in the early 1970s until two wildlife park owners, John Simister and Michael Willis, took it upon themselves to save the Kunekune. They managed to find eighteen pigs that were 'true' Kunes, and began a breeding programme. In the early 1990s Zoe Lindop imported the first of the breed into Great Britain.

Kunes are described by the British Kunekune Pig Society as 'Small, round and hairy, easy to keep, intelligent, grass-eating pigs, ideal for smallholders'. This is an excellent summing up of the breed.

The Kunekune is a relatively small breed, standing between 24 and 30in (60 and 75cm) when full grown. Some people describe their Kunes as 'miniature' or 'small breed', but the truth is that they vary in size quite considerably and there are still many very large Kunekunes that are a testament to the European meat pigs which Captain Cook took on his trips to New Zealand. These pigs crossed with the little Maori pig and the genes are still apt to come through in the breeding now and again. However, it does not follow that a large Kunekune will produce large offspring, or that a small one will produce small offspring.

All pigs have an inclination to root or dig in their search for food, but the little Kunekune is probably the least so inclined. Some do not root at all, and others will only root at certain times of year when the ground is soft and the grass holds little goodness. However, some Kunekunes, it must be said, can root as well as any other breed, and will do so. As a breed they are probably the 'easiest' on your grazing, needing approximately half an acre of ground to keep a couple of them all year round. This amount of land should also be sufficient to rotate them on smaller patches with the help of electric fencing, and preserve the ground or turn it over ready for planting.

The Kunekune is a quiet, gentle-natured and human-friendly little pig. The sow can be prolific, rearing between two and twelve piglets in a litter. She farrows easily, and is a careful and protective mother, although will accept visitors to her farrowing quarters, whether other pigs or people, with equanimity. She is never aggressive.

Being a slow-maturing breed, gilts can be left for as long as two years before going to the boar, although after two years it can become more difficult to breed her for the first time. Sows benefit from a speedy return to the boar after weaning as they are inclined to run to fat, which will prevent them from conceiving a litter.

The New Zealand Kunekune is one of the hardier breeds of pig, being perfectly able to live out all year round with a warm, dry shelter. Their hair not only protects them from the cold but also acts as a sunscreen in the hotter weather. The lighter-skinned pigs will be more susceptible to sunburn and it is always necessary, whatever breed of pig you choose, to provide a good muddy wallow in summer so that your pigs can protect themselves from the sun.

Kunes come in all colours, from the very palest cream through to ginger, brown and black. They can be spotted, patchy or plain in colour, and the coat can vary from thick and curly to fairly sparse and fine. At times a Kunekune will lose its hair, sometimes in small patches and sometimes all over; however, it will grow back again.

Kunekune pig.

As a beginner's breed, the Kunekune is excellent, being small, economical to feed, hardy in weather and against disease, and providing good meat. They are slow growing, and can, unlike the traditional breeds, be finished on little more than grass and a small amount of supplementary food during the winter.

Boars of this breed are also gentle-natured and easy to handle, making them the ideal breed for the beginner. As with the sows and gilts, a bad-natured or aggressive boar should not be bred from. There is currently no AI (artificial insemination) available for Kunekunes but there are many boars at stud.

Kunekune boars will develop 'armour' at around two years of age, similar to that of the wild boar. This comes in the form of an extremely hard and crusty layer of skin – approximately an inch thick – on the shoulders and running the length of the body to the end of the rib cage. This armour is ultimately for protection when fighting in the wild as it can withstand the attack of another boar's tusks.

As with all boars, the Kunekune will develop tusks which will begin to protrude from the sides of the mouth at approximately two years of age.

These can be trimmed right back to the gum by a vet if you feel in any way threatened by them. Although the Kunekune is unlikely to show any aggression with his tusks, they can cause nasty damage by way of an accidental gouge when following close to you, or as a result of boisterous interaction with other pigs during feeding.

One drawback of this breed is that Kunekunes are very inclined to run to fat if not correctly fed, and those carrying excess weight are prone to joint and foot problems.

There is an active breed society for the Kunekune, independent of the British Pig Association. The number of registered Kunekunes now runs into several thousands so the breed is well established, and at the time of writing, the breed society is looking into the possibility of bringing in fresh blood from New Zealand.

The Breed Standard 2010

The breed standard has been updated in 2010 with the intention of representing the diversity of the Kunekune pig and encouraging more healthy features. When judging Kunekunes in the show ring, it is our intention that points be awarded primarily to pigs that are healthy, fit and able to perform the natural functions necessary to survive. The sight should be unobstructed (except by forward-inclined ears), the teeth should be suitable for foraging and grazing, and the overall weight of the pig should be such that it is comfortable and able to run.

The Kunekune's conformation and temperament should have the following characteristics:

Head: The face broad and dished, with a short to medium snout and teeth suitable for grazing.
Ears: Pricked or flopped, and inclined forwards.
Tassels: Two, well formed and well attached.
Neck: Short to medium, with a light to medium jowl (in older animals).
Body: Shoulders level and in proportion, chest moderately wide between the legs, and well rounded hams.
Back: Strong, level or slightly arched.
Tail: A natural tail, set high.
Legs: Straight, well set, able to support the body size. Pasterns short and springy. The ability to walk well with a good straight action.

Feet: Strong, closed and even, bearing in mind the age and size of the Kunekune.

Skin/hair: Healthy, coat may be any colour or texture.

Sexual Characteristics: A sow should have at least ten evenly spaced teats; a boar should exhibit masculine characteristics and also have ten evenly spaced teats.

Temperament: Placid.

Kunekune Bloodlines

Sow: Jenny, Rebecca, Gina, Sally, Kereopa, Awakino, Trish.

Boar: Andrew, Ru, Tutaki, Te Whangi.

THE LARGE BLACK

Breed History

With its lop ears and long, deep body, the Large Black is Britain's only all-black pig. Extremely docile and very hardy, it is ideally suited to simple outdoor systems. These characteristics, coupled with its black skin, make the Large Black ideal for a wide range of climatic conditions – in fact by 1935 pigs of this breed had been exported to well over thirty countries.

The breed originates from the Old English Hog, established in the sixteenth and seventeenth centuries, and described thus by Parkinson in 1810:

> They are distinguished by their gigantic size, they are the largest of the kind I have ever seen, and as perfect a make as possible in pigs; their heads are large, with very long ears hanging down on each side of the face, so they can scarcely see their way.

By the late 1880s there were two distinct types of Large Black, one to be found in East Anglia and the other in Devon and Cornwall. However, the founding of the Large Black Pig Society in 1889 led to an increase in the exchange of stock between breeders in the two regions.

In the early part of the twentieth century, Large Blacks were widely distributed throughout the country and were frequently crossed with Large Whites and Middle Whites to produce bacon and pork pigs. The Large Black breed was also very successful in the show ring at this time; at Smithfield in 1919 the supreme championship was awarded to a Large Black sow that subsequently sold for 700 guineas. The same year the breed outnumbered all other breeds at the Royal Show when 121 Large Black pigs were exhibited.

A change in demand by the meat trade and a developing prejudice against coloured pigs

Large Black pig.

led to a severe decline in numbers throughout the 1960s. Today, however, Large Blacks can be found throughout the British Isles, mainly in small herds, some of which were established well before World War II. Large Black sows are renowned as excellent mothers with exceptional milking ability. They are able to rear sizeable litters off simple rations, and a placid temperament ensures they can be contained behind a single strand of electric fencing.

Current demand for meat produced from traditional breeds of pigs raised extensively is now promoting a growth in the number of breeders keeping Large Blacks, as this particular breed is much appreciated for its succulent taste and eating quality.

Currently the breed has six boar lines and twenty-four sow lines.

The Breed Standard of Excellence

Head: Well proportioned. Medium length, broad and clean between the ears.
Ears: Long, thin and well inclined over the face.
Jowl and cheek: Freedom from the jowl. Strong under-jaw.
Neck: Long and clean.
Chest: Wide and deep.
Shoulders: (Important) Fine and in line with the ribs.
Length: (Of the utmost importance) Good.
Back: Very long and strong.
Loin: Broad and strong.
Ribs: Well sprung.
Sides: Long and moderately deep.
Belly: Full, straight underline, with at least twelve sound, evenly spaced, well placed teats starting well forwards.
Hams: Very broad and full.
Quarters: Long, wide and not drooping.
Tail: Set moderately high and thick set.

Legs: Well set, straight and fat. Fine bone.
Pasterns: Strong.
General movement: Active.
Skin: Blue-black, fine and soft.
Coat: Fine and soft, with moderate quantity of straight black silky hair.
General quality and conformation: Good carriage on sound feet with good length and well developed loin and hams.

Objections

▨ Excessive jowl, narrow forehead, dished or undershot lower jaw
▨ Thick, coarse, cabbage-leafed ears
▨ Coarse, curly or bristly mane
▨ Thick, wrinkled or sooty black skin
▨ Coarse collar
▨ Heavy shoulder, with a coarse shield
▨ Crooked legs, low pasterns and excessively bent hocks
▨ Excessive fat: this should be discouraged at a show

Disqualification

Any other colour than black will disqualify, as will a rose on the back.

THE GLOUCESTERSHIRE OLD SPOT

Breed History

If old paintings are to be trusted spotted pigs have been around for two or three centuries; however, the Gloucestershire Old Spot has only had pedigree status since the early twentieth century. Nevertheless they had been set into type for some time, and were very popular in the Berkeley Vale of Gloucestershire where they were known as the 'orchard pig' since they grazed in the apple orchards, clearing up the windfalls. They lived outside throughout the year, being tough and hardy;

Gloucestershire Old Spot sow and litter. (Courtesy George and Dani Clarke, Hi-Key Studios)

they were also quiet and easily handled, and these qualities are prominent today.

The Gloucestershire Old Spot is a large meaty animal with a broad and deep body and large hams. Its white coat has large, clearly defined black spots. A few years ago fashion called for only one or two spots, but today breeders have decided that if you are going to have a spotted pig, then it should have more spots, and these should be clearly defined, and black not blue. Their legs and feet should be strong and straight, and they should have lop ears that cover the face and come down to the nose.

The Gloucestershire Old Spot is ideally suited to an outdoor system. Provided they have a warm and comfortable hut they will thrive outside all the year round, though this system is better on reasonably dry land that does not become a quagmire in wet weather: the pigs wouldn't mind this, but it would become difficult to get round to look after them. Leading breeder George Styles recalls the occasion one winter when he had Gloucestershire Old Spot sows in outdoor farrowing huts that were well insulated:

> The snow drifted around them and was about a foot deep between 1 January and 1 March. Seventeen sows farrowed and we weaned 173 pigs. It was a wonderful sight to see the little pigs playing in the snow and suckling the sows that were lying in it. Tough as old boots.
>
> Over some thirty years we carried out a concentrated programme of recording and testing. All gilts were ultrasonically tested and boars were tested by PIDA and then MLC at their testing stations. It is interesting to note that several boars had very high testing results and at one stage were the highest of all breeds.

Today the Gloucestershire Old Spot pig has a very fine carcase and produces top quality meat for all purposes, be it pork chops, roasting joints or sausages. Meat of this quality is in demand by the more discerning public, and many butchers are now specializing in it – and this is the breed's future. It is interesting to note that from being a very small breed some forty years ago, it is now the largest numerically of the pig breeds listed by The Rare Breeds Survival Trust and it is going from strength to strength. The breed currently has four male and fifteen female lines.

The Breed Standard of Excellence

Head: Medium length.
Nose: Medium length and slightly dished.
Ears: Well set apart, dropping forwards to the nose, not at the sides, not thick or coarse, and not longer than the nose.
Neck: Medium length with the jowl a little pronounced.
Shoulders: Fine but not raised.
Back: Long and level; should not drop behind the shoulders.
Ribs: Deep, well sprung.
Loin: Very broad.
Sides: Deep, presenting a straight bottom line. Belly and flank should be full and thick. The line from the ribs to the hams should be well filled.
Quarters: Long and wide with a thick tail set well up.
Hams: Large and well filled to the hocks.
Legs: Straight and strong.
Skin: Must not show coarseness or wrinkles.
Coat: Silky and not curly. No mane bristles. Not less than one clean, decisive spot of black hair on black skin; black should not predominate.
Underline: Straight, with a minimum of four-teen sound, evenly spaced and well placed teats starting well forward.

Objections
- Short, thick and elevated ears
- A rose in the coat
- A line of mane bristles
- A sandy colour
- Serious skin wrinkles
- A blue undertone not associated with a spot
- Crooked legs
- A heavy jowl

THE BERKSHIRE

Breed History

Cromwell's troops when quartered in Reading made reference to a locally bred pig renowned for its size and the quality of its bacon and ham. This turned out to be one of the earliest records of the Berkshire breed. These pigs were larger and coarser than today's Berkshire; their colour varied from black to sandy red, and they were sometimes spotted, and had variable white patches. The breed was influenced by the introduction of Chinese and Siamese blood, which resulted in the development of the Berkshire we are familiar with today. This is a smaller animal, black in colour, with prick ears, white socks, a white tip to the tail and a flash on the face.

Important strides in breed improvement took place between 1820 and 1830, much of which is attributed to Lord Barrington. During the nineteenth century the breed became very popular, enjoying patronage from the aristocracy, including Queen Victoria. Its popularity was reflected in the show ring, because by 1877 Smithfield offered separate Berkshire classes, and during the last seventeen years of the eighteenth cen-

Berkshire sow and piglets.

tury, the breed produced twelve Smithfield champions, including pigs exhibited by members of the royal family.

During 1823 the first Berkshire was exported to the USA. This trend continued throughout that century, and at the end of the nineteenth century, herds were also established in Australia and New Zealand. From that time, and during the first half of the twentieth century, the breed grew in popularity, reflected by successes at many leading shows.

But, as with all coloured pig breeds, the Berkshire suffered a serious decline in popularity following World War II, when the demand for leaner bacon from white-skinned pigs increased, and then in the 1960s with the development of breeding companies that favoured white breeds. Nevertheless, due to a few loyal stalwarts, the Berkshire survived. Today's increasing interest in traditional meat produced extensively has renewed interest in the breed. Although it is a coloured breed the meat dresses out white; also it is an early finishing breed, so an ideal carcase weighs between 36kg and 45kg (79 and 99lb).

A number of breeders have developed their own specialized markets for Berkshire pig meat, and Berkshire breeding stock are also in demand overseas – especially in Japan –

where the breed is very popular and is marketed as 'black pork' at a premium price. Japanese buyers still consider Berkshires from Britain to have the best taste and flavour.

Six boars have been imported over the past fifty years from Australia and New Zealand, and semen has also been sourced from the USA. These importations of grading up three female lines have helped broaden the breed's genetic base, and today there are six male and nine female bloodlines available to breeders.

The Breed Standard of Excellence

Character: A combination of the following definitions denoting type, quality, breeding and masculinity in the case of boars, and femininity in the case of sows and gilts.

Head: Fine, face dished, snout of medium length, wide between the eyes and ears. Ears fairly large, carried erect or slightly inclined forward and fringed with fine hair. Jowl light.

Middle White pig. (Courtesy George and Dani Clarke, Hi-Key Studios)

Neck: Fine, evenly set on the shoulders, free from wrinkles and free from crest.

Shoulders: Fine and well sloping. Special notice to be taken regarding this point in the case of females.

Legs and feet: Straight and strong, set wide apart, standing well on the toes; should be a good walker.

Back: Long and level; tail set high; good spring of rib.

Hams: Broad, wide and deep to the hock.

Belly: Straight underline, with at least twelve (preferably fourteen) sound, evenly spaced and well placed teats starting well forwards.

Bone: Well developed in males and fine in females.

Flesh: Firm without excessive fat.

Skin: Fine and free from wrinkles.

Hair: Long, fine and plentiful, with no mane, especially in females.

Colour: Black, with white on the face, feet and tip of the tail only.

Objections
- A crooked jaw
- In-bent knees
- Rose in the coat

THE MIDDLE WHITE

Breed History

The Middle White was first recognized as a breed in 1852 in most unusual circumstances. At the Keighley Agricultural Show in West Yorkshire, Joseph Tuley, a weaver by trade, exhibited several of his famous Large White sows along with other pigs. However, some of the animals were considered to be not large enough for the class, and the judges could not agree; but 'as the merits of these pigs were so extraordinary, entirely forbidding recourse to disqualification, a committee was summoned, whereupon the judges declaring that, if removed from the Large White class the pigs would not be eligible for the Small White class', it was decided to provide a third class and to call it the 'Middle Breed'. In this way the 'Middle White' breed was established.

The Small White had been developed for showing and had derived from crossing the local pigs with imported Chinese and Siamese pigs, from which it inherited the dished face, so much the characteristic of the Middle White.

In further establishing the Middle White breed, Tuley took a second cross with a boar of the Small White breed and females from the best type of Large White in his herd. The resulting progeny were as heavy as the pure Large White, although in type and lightness of offal and head they much resembled the best of the Small White breed. The Small White became extinct in 1912.

Due to the 'new' breed's eating qualities, its early maturing and its very easy management, the Middle White went from strength to strength. When the National Pig Breeders Association was founded in 1884 the Middle White along with the Large White and Tamworth were the three foundation breeds, and their first herd books were published that same year. The Middle White remained very popular with butchers everywhere, particularly in London where the breed was known as 'the London Porker' because the carcases could be cut into the small joints favoured in the first part of the twentieth century.

World War II and meat rationing until 1954 led to a concentration on the 'bacon' pig, and the specialist pork pig was sidelined. Along with other 'pork' breeds the number of Middle Whites declined sharply during this period, though fortunately a number of dedicated breeders ensured the continuation of the breed. In recent years the demand for meat

with good eating qualities has once again led to Middle White pork appearing on the menus of top London restaurants, with 'glowing reports' regarding its outstanding quality.

Middle White breeding stock has been exported worldwide, and the breed is particularly appreciated in Japan where they are known as 'Middle Yorks'. The Middle White has many assets: in particular it is docile and very easily managed, and it can make a positive contribution to cross-breeding programmes to improve eating quality.

The Middle White Pig Breeders Club was established in 1990 and has as its patron the well known chef Antony Worrall Thompson, whose enthusiasm for the breed has led him to breed his own Middle White pigs.

The Breed Standard of Excellence

Character: A combination of the following definitions denotes type, quality, breeding and sex characteristics.

Head: Moderately short, face dished, snout broad, jaw straight, jowl light, eyes set well apart, wide between the ears, which should be fairly large and inclined forwards and outwards and fringed with fine hair.

Neck: Fairly light, of medium length, proportionately and evenly set on the shoulders.

Shoulders: Fine, sloping and aligned with the legs and sides. Free from coarseness.

Back: Long and level to the root of the tail with well sprung ribs.

Sides: Deep and level.

Belly: Thick and straight underline, with at least twelve (preferably fourteen) sound, evenly spaced, well placed teats starting well forwards.

Hams: Broad and deep to the hock.

Tail: Set high, with no depression at the root, moderately long but not coarse, with a tassel of fine hair.

Legs: Straight and fairly short, well set apart, bone fine and flat, pasterns short and springy, standing well up on the toes; should be a good walker.

Skin: Free from coarseness, wrinkles and spots.

Hair: Should be of fine quality.

Objections

The use of artificial whitening for the removal of spots by artificial means is prohibited.

Disqualifications

▧ Rose on the back
▧ Extra toes
▧ A twisted jaw

THE SADDLEBACK

Breed History

The British Saddleback is the result of the amalgamation of two similar breeds, the

British Saddleback pig. (Courtesy Debbie and David Beeby)

Essex and Wessex Saddleback. The origin of the Improved Essex pig is better authenticated than most. Lord Western, while travelling in Italy, saw some Neapolitan pigs and came to the conclusion that they were just what he needed to improve the breed of Essex pigs. He procured a pair of Neapolitans and crossed them with Essex sows. One of his tenants, Fisher Hobbs of Boxted Lodge, availed himself of the opportunity to use the Neapolitan-Essex boars belonging to Lord Western, and crossed them with his coarse Essex sows: in the course of time he established the Improved Essex. Sidney, in his last edition of *Youatt on the Pig*, says:

> The improved Essex probably date their national reputation from the second show of the Royal Agricultural Society, held at Cambridge in 1840, when a boar and sow, both bred by Mr Hobbs, each obtained first prizes in their respective classes.

The Essex pig was mainly found in East Anglia. This pig had a black head and neck, as well as a clearly defined belt of white extending over the shoulders and continuing over the forelegs. The rest of the body was black, with the exception of white feet and the tip of the tail.

The Wessex originated in the New Forest as a cross between two indigenous old English bacon pigs. By 1914 the breed was also found in the South and the South West. It was black all over, apart from a continuous belt of white hair over the forelegs and shoulder. W. J. Walden, writing in the 1931 NPBA Gazette, explains that stringent rules were put in place by the Wessex Saddleback Pig Society at its foundation to prevent alien blood being brought in where the foundation on one side was not of New Forest origin. The breed prided itself on having resisted the trend to introduce Chinese blood. In his article on Wessex Saddleback markings Walden asks:

> Why then make a feature of the chief colouration marking? Surely it does not take a high intelligence to see the correctness and advantage of the one conspicuous trade mark when two China free breeds are brought together?

The respective breed societies amalgamated in 1918 and the herd books followed suit in 1967 when the British Saddleback breed was established. The two breeds enjoyed great popularity during World War II when 47 per cent of the total pedigree sow registrations were from the Essex and Wessex breed. In 1949 there were 2,435 Essex and Wessex boars licensed, representing almost 25 per cent of the licensed boars for that year. The sows retained some of their popularity in the postwar years. In 1954 they made up 22 per cent of the total registrations for that year. The boars, however, had lost considerable ground to white breeds, and in the same year less than 10 per cent of the licensed boars were from the Essex and Wessex breeds. The recommendations of the time were to cross sows of either breed with a white boar to produce a dual-purpose pig for combined pork and bacon production.

British Saddlebacks are hardy and renowned for their grazing ability, and noted for their mothering ability. The breed continues to be used mainly to provide coloured dams for the production of first-cross porkers, baconers and heavy pigs. It has secured a niche in outdoor and organic production. Many Saddlebacks have been exported to Nigeria and the Seychelles where the pigs have performed well on coarse grazing in hot climatic conditions.

The Breed Standard of Excellence

Colour: Black and white but with a continuous belt of white hair encircling the shoulders and forelegs. White is permissible on the nose, the tip of the tail and on the hind legs but no higher than the hock.
Head: Medium length, face very slightly dished, under-jaw clean cut and free from jowl. Medium width between the ears.
Ears: Medium size, carried forward, curbing but not obscuring the vision.
Neck: Clean and of medium length.
Shoulders: Medium width, free from coarseness, not too deep.
Chest: Wide and not too deep.
Back: Long and straight.
Loin: Broad, strong and free from slackness.
Ribs: Well sprung.
Sides: Long and of medium depth.
Hams: Broad, full and well filled to the hocks.
Underline: Straight with at least twelve sound, evenly spaced and well placed teats starting well forwards.
Legs: Strong with good bone, straight, well set on each corner of the body.
Feet: Strong and of good size.
Coat: Fine, silky and straight.
Action: Firm and free.

Disqualification
- An animal not possessing a continuous band of white hair over the shoulders and forelegs
- Rose on the back or shoulder
- Chocolate or red-coloured skin

Objectionable Features
- Badger face, short or up-turned snout

- Pricked or floppy ears
- Curly or coarse coat, coarse mane
- Coarse or wrinkled skin
- Unsound or unevenly placed teats

TAMWORTH

Breed History

Today's Tamworth is thought to be the most typical breed descended from the old indigenous species, the Old English Forest pig. It has maintained this status because at the end of the eighteenth century when many native breeds were 'improved' by crossing them with Chinese and Neapolitan stock, the Tamworth was not deemed fashionable and hence was left alone. It is now therefore the oldest pure English breed, and as a result it is also sometimes crossed with wild boar to produce distinctive gamey pork.

During the twentieth century Tamworths

Tamworth pig.

were both exported and imported, an exercise vitally important to a breed with small numbers and potential inbreeding problems. During the early part of the century the imports were predominantly from Canada, one famous one being 'Dollar Bobbie' whose progeny resulted in the Rose line (no relation to the modern-day Golden Rose).

The red-gold hair of the Tamworth ensures that it is one of the most easily recognizable of the traditional pig breeds. A typical Tamworth has the longest snout of the present-day domestic breeds. It has prick ears, giving it an alert appearance. This reflects its inquisitive nature, a characteristic enforcing its reputation for speed in the show ring.

A Tamworth's head should not be too long – the face should be slightly dished and wide between the ears, with a light jowl. The large ears are finely fringed and carried slightly inclined. The skin should be flesh coloured and free from coarseness, wrinkles or black spots. The coat is distinctively golden red, abundant, straight, fine and as free of black hairs as possible.

The sows are excellent mothers, being milky, docile as well as protective. As with all traditional breeds, the Tamworth is hardy and can be kept in environments ranging from rough pasture to meadowland. Of all the native breeds it is particularly resistant to sunburn.

Well over a century ago, when landowners, farmers, hotel keepers and cottagers kept pigs to cure their own bacon, the Tamworth enjoyed popularity because it produced a white-fleshed carcase with long sides and big hams. As the breed's name suggests, these pigs are traditionally remembered as cottagers' pigs in the Midlands.

After World War II, breeding stock numbers fell dramatically, to a point during the 1970s when there were only seventeen surviving boars. At this time it was felt that the Canadian pigs were a darker red than was preferred and the breed turned to Australia for its importations, a country that had previously imported from Britain. The Rare Breeds Survival Trust continued this tradition with two importations. In 1976 several boars were imported from the Royal Standard, Golden Ranger and Glen lines, and in the late 1990s the importation was of both boars and gilts. On this occasion the boars were incorporated into all the female lines and a further female line, 'Rita', was established.

The Breed Standard of Excellence

Coat: Golden red, abundant, straight and fine, and as free from black hairs as possible.
Head: Not too long, face slightly dished, wide between the ears, jowl light.
Ears: Rather large with a fine fringe, carried rigid and slightly inclined.
Neck: Light, medium length, proportionately and evenly set on the shoulders.
Chest: Well sprung and not too deep.
Shoulders: Light, free from coarseness, in alignment with the forelegs below and with the side as seen from in front.
Legs: Strong and shapely, with good quality bone and set well outside the body; pasterns short and springy, standing well up on the toe.
Back: Long and deep.
Sides: Long and of medium depth.
Loin: Strong and broad.
Tail: Set high and well tasselled.
Belly: Straight underline with at least twelve sound, evenly spaced and well placed teats starting well forwards.
Flank: Full and well let down.
Hams: Well developed with plenty of width and giving a firm appearance.
Skin: Flesh coloured, free from coarseness, wrinkles or black spots.
Action: Firm and free.

Objection
▧ Black hairs growing from black spots

Note: When exhibiting Tamworth pigs, oil should not be used.

THE WELSH

Breed History

The earliest references to a Welsh pig come from the 1870s when there was a considerable trade in Welsh and Shropshire pigs into Cheshire for fattening on milk by-products.

> The Welsh pigs are generally a yellow-white, but some are spotted black and white. The [Cheshire] dairymen depend more on these Welshmen and proud Salopians than on breeding. The cross of the Manchester boar with the Shropshire and Welsh produces a larger and coarser breed than the small Yorkshire.

Increased demand for pork and bacon during World War I, when imports were restricted to Canada and the USA, led to the creation of the first pig breed society in Wales. The Old Glamorgan Pig Society was established in 1918. Volume 1 of the herd book was published in 1919. Pigs of a similar type were also bred in Cardigan, Pembroke and Camarthen. A meeting was held at Carmarthen in 1920 resulting in the foundation of the Welsh Pig Society in West Wales. The first herd book was published in 1922.

These two breed societies amalgamated in 1922 to become the Welsh Pig Society, with offices at Shire Hall in Camarthen. In 1923 Volume 4 of the Old Glamorgan Pig Society herd book and Volume 2 of the Welsh herd book were published separately. Volume 5 published in 1924 was the first issued as the

Welsh pig.

Welsh Pig Society. In 1952 the Welsh breed joined the six other pedigree breeds already represented by the National Pig Breeders Association, now known as the British Pig Association (BPA). The first NPBA herd book containing entries for Welsh pigs was published in 1953.

The Welsh breed prospered greatly during the period from 1947 when increasing supplies of animal feed led to a dramatic increase in the national pig herd. The number of government licenses issued for Welsh boars increased from forty-one in 1949 to 1,363 in 1954, making the Welsh the number three sire breed in Great Britain behind the Large White and Landrace. A similar picture existed for pedigree sow registrations, which rose from 850 in 1952 to 3,736 in 1954.

The Howitt Committee – established in 1955 to advise government on future breeding policy, and which included amongst its members the eminent scientist Dr J. Hammond – identified the Welsh as one of the three breeds on which the modern British pig industry should be founded. 'It is from these three breeds we would hope to see developed, through intensive progeny testing in the coming years, the improved bacon pig which would provide boars for use by nearly all commercial breeders for bacon and pork.'

Nucleus herds of Welsh pigs were established as part of the national testing scheme, and throughout the 1960s and 1970s the breed was the third most numerous in the testing programmes. The *1974/75 Pig Improvement Scheme Year Book* shows performance figures on a par with the other two breeds selected by the Howitt committee. During this period the Welsh breed was widely used in commercial herds. At the same time, breeders with a slightly different type of Welsh pig were winning awards in the show ring. At Smithfield and other prime stock shows the breed enjoyed numerous successes in both the pork and bacon sectors.

The Welsh pig is white, with lop ears meeting at the tips just short of the pig's nose. It has a long, level body with deep, strong hams and legs set well apart. George Eglington, acknowledged as the founder of the modern Welsh breed, described the perfect Welsh pig as 'pear shaped' when viewed from either the side or from above. They are still known for their hardiness and ability to thrive under a wide variety of conditions, both indoor and outside.

Since the 1980s the number of registrations has declined; however, the breed still provides a valuable source of genetic material for breeders following crossbreeding programmes. They make for ease of management with a fast liveweight gain at a low feed conversion ratio, and an excellent killing out percentage in the progeny.

Currently the breed has fourteen boar lines and thirty-two sow lines.

The Breed Standard of Excellence

Head: Light, fine and fairly wide between the ears, which should tend to meet at the tips short of the nose.

Nose: Straight and clean jowl.

Neck: Clean and not too deep.

Shoulders: Light, but with the forelegs set well apart, somewhat flat-topped, and the shoulder leading into really well sprung ribs. Lack of depth down through the shoulders and chest is most important.

Back: Long, strong and level with well sprung ribs giving a fairly wide mid-back. The tail should be thick and free from depressions at the root.

Loin: Should be well muscled, firm and well developed, the belly and flank to be thick, the underline straight.

Hindquarters: Strong with hams full, firm and thick, whether viewed from the back or sides, and full to the hocks but not flabby.

Legs: Of adequate length, straight and set well apart with short pasterns and good strong bone.

Coat: Straight and fine. Roses and crown back are undesirable.

Skin: Fine and free from wrinkles.

Teats: At least fourteen sound and evenly placed teats on both boars and females.

Colour: White, blue spots undesirable.

Action: Should be active, alert and move freely and easily.

THE OXFORD SANDY AND BLACK

Breed History

The Oxford Sandy and Black pig is sometimes referred to as the 'Plum Pudding or Oxford Forest' pig and is one of the oldest British pig breeds: it has existed for 200–300 years. It is a traditional farmer's and cottager's pig deriving from the middle part of the country, especially around Oxfordshire. It seems to be closely linked to the old Berkshire and Tamworth, but no one is entirely sure whether it diverged from them, or was the result of crossbreeding between them – or indeed was the result of crossbreeding with an entirely different breed altogether.

The Oxford Sandy and Black – or OSB – has reached crisis point at least twice in its past when numbers dropped so low that extinction was a real possibility. Unfortunately it had no society or herd book to look after its wellbeing. As long ago as the 1940s boar licensing had dropped to one or two a year for OSBs, and but for a few dedicated breeders the breed would surely have been lost. In 1973 the Rare Breeds Survival Trust was formed, giving hope for the breed – but the Trust decided not to recognize the OSB. Once again the dedicated breeders were on their

Oxford Sandy and Black pig. (Courtesy Liz Shankland)

own, but the OSB continued to decline to the brink of extinction. Fortunately in 1985 the current breed society was formed, the society's founder secretary Steven Kimmins having made contact with all known breeders of the OSB; he was ably supported and helped by Andrew J. Sheppy, chairman, and Geoffrey Cloke, president, and the OSB owes its survival to these people.

There were twenty-nine herds listed in the first herd book, with fifteen boars and sixty-two sows. Sadly some of the bloodlines have been lost, but today's dedicated and enthusiastic breeders are determined to save the remaining lines. The current picture is very encouraging, with the rarest bloodlines hanging on and slowly increasing. Even though OSBs are still relatively few in number, the breed is now recognized by the BPA, and this has hopefully secured its future: herd book management has been transferred to the BPA from the Oxford Sandy and Black Society, and this recognition has already brought the hoped-for benefits of increased publicity and the opportunity to compete in the shop window of BPA-recognized shows.

The bloodlines are:

- Boars: Alexander, Alistair, Clarence, Jack
- Sows: Alison, Clare, Clarissa, Cynthia, Dandy, Duchess, Elsie, Gertrude, Gloria, Iris, Lady, Mary, Sybil

The breed has many good qualities, particularly its excellent temperament and mothering abilities. Prolific and hardy and a good forager, it is particularly suited to outdoor systems, and because it is a coloured pig with a good coat it is far less prone to sunburn.

The OSB is a medium to large pig with good length and a deep body, good quarters and fine shoulders, and strong, well set on legs and feet, giving a free and active gait. It

has a moderately strong head with a straight or slightly dished face and lop or semi-lop ears. In colour it is light sandy to rust, with random black blotches (not spots), and a white blaze, feet and tassel. It produces fine quality, white-skinned pork and bacon with a superb flavour, and will finish to pork weight in twenty-two weeks.

The Breed Standard of Excellence

Size: Medium to large.
Body: Long and deep with broad hindquarters and rather finer forequarters.
Back: Slightly arched, strong and well sprung.
Head: Moderately long with a slightly dished muzzle; a short or very dished face is a defect.
Ears: Medium, semi-lop to full lop – that is, carried horizontally or lower; erect ears are unacceptable.
Legs: Medium length, strong boned and well set on, giving a free and active gait.
Colour: Ground colour sandy, markings black in random blotches rather than small spots, with sandy the predominant colour; pale feet, blaze and tassel are characteristic.

THE DUROC

Breed History

In 1812, early 'Red Hogs' were bred in New York and New Jersey. They were large in size, and large litters and the ability to grow quickly were characteristics that Durocs possessed from the beginning. The foundation stock that produced today's 'Duroc' comprised Red Durocs from New York and Jersey Reds from New Jersey. In 1823, Isaac Frink of Milton in Saratoga County, New York, obtained from Harry Kelsey of Florida, New

*Duroc pig.
(Courtesy
Liz
Shankland)*

York, a red boar, one of a litter of ten pigs. The sire and dam of these pigs were probably imported from England. Kelsey owned a famous trotting stallion named Duroc, so Frink named his red boar in honour of the horse. This boar was known for his smoothness and carcase quality.

His progeny continued the Duroc name, and many of them inherited his colour, quick growth and maturity, deep body, broad ham and shoulder, and quiet disposition. The Duroc was smaller than the Jersey Red, with finer bones and better carcase quality. Beginning in the early 1860s, the Duroc evolved from a systematic blending of the two very different strains.

The first organization for the purpose of recording, improving and promoting Red Hogs was the American Duroc-Jersey Association, established in 1883. At the 1893 Chicago World's Fair, Durocs gained wide popularity at the first successful Duroc Hog Show.

The Duroc made two attempts to gain a foothold in the UK: the first in the early 1970s was not very successful, although some of those pigs were exported on to Denmark. They were re-imported in the early 1980s, and a comprehensive trial was undertaken by the MLC to assess the merits of the Duroc as a terminal sire. It was found that in the British 'skin-on' fresh pork market the Duroc could not be used as a purebred, but only as a component of a crossbred boar. The development of Duroc crossbred boars produced large numbers of crossbred gilts, and a market was found for these due to a resurgence of interest in outdoor pig production. This has resulted in breeding and selection programmes for the British Duroc focusing on female line characteristics rather than the traditional terminal sire traits associated with the breed. The Duroc has now found a special niche in the British industry, and a unique British version of the breed has been developed.

The Duroc's thick auburn winter coat and hard skin enables it to survive the cold and wet of the British winter. This coat moults out in summer to leave the pig looking almost bald, but as a consequence it can cope with hot, dry summers equally well. All purebred Durocs are red in colour, and the development of a so-called 'White Duroc' has only been achieved by crossbreeding with a white breed.

Its tenacity in looking after its young combined with its docility between times makes it an ideal candidate for an outdoor pig, either as a dam or sire line, and its succulence and heavy muscling makes it very suitable for anything from light pork to heavy hog production.

Further research funded by the MLC has investigated the Duroc's claim to produce high levels of tenderness. This has led to a recommendation to include Duroc genetics as part of the meat quality blueprint.

The Breed Standard of Excellence

Head and face: Head small in proportion to the size of the body, wide between the eyes, face nicely dished and tapering well down to the nose; surface smooth and even.

Eyes: Lively, bright and prominent.

Ears: Medium, moderately thin, pointing forwards, downwards and slightly outwards, and carrying a slight curve.

Neck: Short, thick, very deep and slightly arching.

Jowl: Broad, full and neat.

Shoulders: Moderately broad, very deep and full, carrying thickness well down and not extending above the line of the back.

Chest: Large, very deep, full behind the shoulders, breastbone extending well forwards so readily seen.

Back and loin: Back medium in breadth, straight or slightly arching, carrying even width from shoulder to ham, giving the impression of a slightly low-set tail; surface even and smooth.

Legs and feet: Of medium length, with good strong bone (especially boars).

Sides and ribs: Sides very deep, medium in length, level between the shoulders and hams; ribs long, strong and sprung in proportion to the width of the shoulders and hams.

Belly and flank: Flank well down to the lower line of the sides; underline straight with at least twelve sound teats placed well forwards.

Hams and rump: Broad, full and well let down to the hock; rumps should have a round slope from the loin to the root of the tail.

Hair: Thick in winter, fine in summer, no coarse and curly hair.

Gait: Free and fluid.

Colour: Skin white or pink, at worst light grey; hair auburn.

Disqualification

The following traits will lead to disqualification from the herd book:

- Ears standing erect
- Small cramped chest
- Crease at the back of the shoulders and over back so as to cause an easily noticed depression in the back
- Seriously deformed legs
- Badly broken down feet
- Very small stature, or more specifically: not two-thirds large enough as given by the standard
- White in any of the hair

THE HAMPSHIRE

Breed History

The Hampshire has been developed in the United States of America and is now one of the world's most important breeds. In some respects, however, it can be regarded as a British native breed, as the original breeding stock was imported from Wessex in 1832, the date being recorded in the Hampshire Blue Book published in 1928. The book records the complete history of the breed and its origin.

From the time of its arrival in the USA until 1890 the breed was called the 'Thin Rind' breed, due to the abundance of lean meat it produced. Then at a meeting of American breeders in 1890 the breed was renamed the Hampshire, because the original pigs were imported from a farm in Hampshire, Wessex, UK. A breed society was established at the same time, and herd book recording can be traced for more than 100 years.

The Hampshire is used extensively as the sire of cross-bred pigs for the pork and manufacturing markets in the USA and many other countries. It has the reputation of being the leanest of the North American breeds, and the majority of carcase competitions in North America are won by Hampshires and Hampshire crosses.

The first Hampshires to return to the UK were imported from the USA in 1968 by the Animal Breeding Research Organization (ABRO). The import was a 'random sample' of the breed, and the pigs were extensively performance tested before being released to British breeders.

The next major importation was in 1973 when forty pigs from many different USA bloodlines were brought in from Canada (import restrictions at that time prohibited

Hampshire pig. (Courtesy Liz Shankland)

direct imports from the USA). This importation was very carefully selected, and included a boar that was grand champion at the 1972 Toronto Royal Show. This same boar was breed champion at the English Royal Show in 1975.

British Hampshires very soon became popular worldwide, and in a twelve-month period – from August 1978 to August 1979 – more than 600 head were exported to fourteen different countries. The British Hampshire, both purebred and crosses, has won many interbreed championships at the Royal Smithfield Show, London, for carcases and live pigs. During the 1980s and 1990s several new bloodlines were imported from the USA by embryo transfer and boar semen.

In the world of commercial pig production there is certainly a place for the Hampshire, still regarded by many as the best terminal sire breed for all purposes.

The Breed Standard of Excellence

Head: Medium size, wide between the eyes

British Lop pig. (Courtesy Tracey Jaine, Northmoor Rare)

and ears; boars to show masculine characteristics, sows feminine.

Ears: Erect or inclined slightly forwards; avoid ears that are too small.

Jowl: As clean as possible.

Chest: Wide between the front legs giving plenty of heart room.

Shoulders: Strong and clean, avoiding the apex top.

Sides: Long and deep, particularly through the heart.

Flank: Trim but well let down.

Underline: Straight; at least twelve sound, evenly spaced, well placed teats, starting well forwards.

Back and loin: Well sprung ribs, smooth long muscle.

Ham and rump: Wide, long front to rear, deep from top to bottom; smooth muscle, tail set high.

Feet and legs: Strong, flat bone, medium length; straight, set well apart and on all four corners; avoid short legs. Strong feet with short cleys of equal length; pasterns short and springy.

Movement: Should be loose in every way with no sign of tightness.

Colour: Predominantly black, but must have a saddle of white skin and white front legs.

General

The Hampshire breeding animal should give the overall impression of scope, and breeders should be looking for large, strong-boned animals as the prime purpose of the Hampshire in the United Kingdom and elsewhere is to produce boars to act as terminal sires.

THE BRITISH LOP

Breed History

The British Lop is a West Country breed which originated around the Tavistock area either side of the Cornwall/Devon borders. For most of its history from the early years of the twentieth century it remained a local breed undiscovered by farmers outside its native territory. It suited the locality well and was in strong demand there, so there was little incentive for breeders to go shouting its merits beyond the far South West. In those days it was registered and known as the 'National Long White Lop-Eared' breed – certainly descriptive if not very snappy. In the 1960s the name was changed to today's 'British Lop'.

When the Rare Breeds Survival Trust (RBST) was established in 1973, the Lop was listed as one of the six rare pig breeds recognized by them. The inclusion of a breed officially listed as 'rare' generally increased interest in all such breeds, and indeed the Lop is more populous now than at any time in the last thirty or so years. However, by comparison with the other rare breeds of pig, it suffered by not looking particularly distinctive. It is, after all, simply a white lop-eared pig, as its earlier name describes, and to the non-specialist could be confused with the Welsh or the Landrace. Enthusiasts flocked to pigs with short snouts, and to spotted or ginger hogs, but not so readily to a pig that looked quite normal.

Yet the Lop has a great deal going for it. It is generally docile and easy to manage, and is hardy enough for outdoor systems. It grows readily, and will finish with a well muscled, lean carcase at pork or bacon weights. The dams are prolific and make good, milky mothers.

So whether for larger production systems, or for smallholders looking for an easily managed breed to produce good quality meat for the growing niche market, the Lop will do the job, and will do it better than most: it is indeed the breed for every need.

The Advantages of the British Lop

- The British Lop is docile and easily managed
- Being a white pig, it does not suffer from the commercial bias against coloured pigs
- It is an excellent mother pig
- It is suitable for both small-scale and extensive commercial systems
- The pork and bacon from a well finished Lop is a high quality product that attracts niche market opportunities
- Unlike some rare breeds, the Lop does not tend to run to excessive fat if poorly managed

By choosing to keep pedigree British Lops, you will be helping to conserve one of the rarest British breeds.

THE LANDRACE

Breed History

The first Landrace pigs were imported into Britain from Sweden in 1949 (four boars and eight gilts), with other imports following from 1953 onwards: these came into Northern Ireland, the Isle of Man and the Channel Islands. The British Landrace Pig Society was formed to create a herd book for the first offspring born in 1950 from the 1949 importation, and an evaluation scheme was created, with the first pig testing scheme for daily gain and fat depths: a testing station

British Landrace pig. (Courtesy Liz Shankland)

was built at Stockton-on-Forest, York. This was a first example of pig testing in the UK, and a testament to the foresight of the founder members of the society as to the future needs in commercial and pedigree pig production.

With an eye on the development of the pedigree pig industry and the need for a national herd book for all breeds, in 1978 the British Landrace Pig Society joined forces with NPBA, now the British Pig Association.

New bloodlines were imported into England, Scotland and Northern Ireland from Norway in the 1980s, and some new blood-lines into Northern Ireland from Finland and more recently from Norway. These new lines were imported and assessed, and used to broaden the genetic base of the breed, allow-ing development, and making the British Landrace pig unique amongst other Landrace breeds throughout the world.

The British Landrace breed has expanded rapidly to occupy its present position as one of the UK's most popular breeds of pig. Landrace breeders are acutely aware of the need to improve the commercial attributes of the breed, carrying on from the 1950s with testing and selection right up to the present day, thus keeping up with the demands of the ever-changing world of commercial/pedigree pig production.

The British Landrace is a very versatile breed, performing well under either indoor or outdoor systems of management. Sows have the ability to produce and rear large litters of piglets with very good daily gain; they have a high-lean meat content in a superbly fleshed carcase, which is ideal for either fresh pork or bacon production.

The greatest strength of the Landrace is its undisputed ability to improve other breeds of pig when crossed to produce hybrid gilts – over 90 per cent of hybrid gilt production in Western Europe and North America uses Landrace bloodlines as the foundation for the profitable production of quality pig meat.

The Breed Standard of Excellence

Head and neck: Head light, of medium length and fine, with minimum jowl and a straight nose (slightly concave with age); neck clean and light, and of medium length.

Ears: Medium in size, neither coarse nor heavy, drooping and slanting forward.

Shoulders: Not deep, free from coarseness, of adequate width and well laid into the body.

Back: Long and slightly arched; breadth uniform throughout, with no dip at the shoul-ders or loin.

Sides and ribs: Sides firm, compact and not deep; well sprung ribs throughout.

Loin: Strong and wide with no deficiency in muscle; no dip in front of the hams.

Hindquarters and hams: Hindquarters of medium length, broad, straight or very slightly sloping to the tail. Hams full and rounded from both back and sides, deep to the hock, wide between the legs with a moderately good inner thigh.

Tail: Set reasonably high, thick at the root.

Belly: Should be straight, with at least four-teen sound, well placed teats, starting well forward.

Legs, feet and pasterns: Legs of medium length, well set on and square with the body, the bone strong but not coarse. Cleys should be even and well developed; pasterns strong, springy and not too long.

Action: Firm and free.

Skin and hair: Skin soft and slightly pink; hair fine and white.

General

The Landrace pig has been developed for speed of growth to furnish a long, lean carcase whilst preserving stamina and a strong constitution.

THE MANGALITZA

Breed History

The pig illustrated is a Mangalitza or Woolly Pig, found in Austria, Germany, Hungary, Romania and Switzerland. The whole Mangalitza breed was almost lost, with the total population worldwide down to fewer than 150 sows in 1993. Thanks to the work of a small group of dedicated breeders, the Mangalitza has been brought back from the verge of extinction; it is now farmed on large units in Hungary and has been exported to North America as well as the UK.

Imported into the UK in 2006, there are seven female lines and three boar lines established. There are three distinct types within the breed: the Blonde, the Red and the unique Swallow-bellied with white underline. All three types are very hardy. The Swallow-bellied Mangalitza was developed in the 1800s from crossing the Blonde with the Black Mangalitza. Unfortunately the Black pig became extinct in the 1970s, the last known herd being on the Serb islands in the Danube. The Mangalitza is a fairly primitive breed, lively and friendly, with strong maternal instincts. Litter sizes are currently not large, averaging about six.

Once renowned as a lard pig capable of producing 70ltr of rendered fat, the Mangalitza has carved out new niche markets in forestry projects and in the production of special hams and salamis. The breed was featured at the Salone Del Gusto in Turin in 2004. The meat is well marbled so is tastier and less dry than that from more modern breeds, and the fat is also special in that

Mangalitza pig. (Courtesy Tracey Jaine, Northmoor Rare Breeds)

it has a higher level of monounsaturated fats: this means that it goes rancid less easily, which is good for a long curing process. It also has a healthier balance of Omega 3 to Omega 6 fatty acids than seed oils, which have become so popular in modern cookery.

The Mangalitza is an unusual, very attractive breed, and has a serious contribution to make as a specialist food product.

The Breed Standard of Excellence

Head: Medium wide, with the bridge of the cylindrical nose a little dented; face and jaws are hairy and meaty, the neck is short.
Ears: Generally lop, medium to large, rounded and droopy, hanging forward; in the red variety they are upright.
Hair: Dense and long, frilled in winter, softer, shorter and straighter in the summer: the seasonal change is characteristic in healthy, well tended animals.
Skin: Grey – black pigment: the mouth, hooves and teats are black. A feature is 'the well-man spot', a bright area of skin, usually around the ear, 3–5cm (1–2in) in diameter, which merges with the pigmented hide.
Eyes: Brown with black eyebrows and eyelashes.
Tail: Usually white with a black interior; if red-haired the tail is also red.
Teats: A minimum of five, well placed, and sound on both sides.
Torso: A fine, very robust skeleton with a straight back with possibly a slight curve to the short/medium hams.
Dimensions: Height 70–90cm (27–35in), length (root of the tail to back of the head behind the ears) 120–140cm (47–54in); weight is perhaps 70–80kg (154–176lb) after one year, 80–100kg (176–220lb) after two years, and up to 300kg (660lb) when fattened and fully grown.

General
The Mangalitza is of medium height, and varies in colour from blonde, through red to swallow-bellied (black above and white below).

Objections
- Pink on the belly skin and under the hair on the torso
- Dark brown tips to the hair, and black or brown bristles
- Ears that are too long

Forbidden for Breeding
- Generally spotted torso or head
- Grey or yellow hooves
- Pink teats

THE LARGE WHITE

Breed History

First recognized in 1868, the Large White owes its origins to the old Yorkshire breed. The Large White was one of the original founder breeds of the National Pig Breeders' Association (now known as the British Pig Association), and the first herd book was published in 1884. Large Whites are distinguished by their erect ears and slightly dished faces. They are long-bodied with excellent hams and fine white hair, and as their name suggests, they are characterized by their large size.

The early history of the breed in Yorkshire is difficult to trace. The large, coarse-boned and leggy white pigs of the region were crossed with other breeds. Davidson, in *The Production and Marketing of Pigs*, has suggested that among these were the Cumberland, Leicestershire and the Middle and Small White. Specimens of the new breed first attracted attention at the Windsor Royal Show

Large White pig. (Courtesy Liz Shankland)

in 1831; however, the stock used in the development and improvement of the pigs of that area is not as important as what was finally produced as a breed.

Before the end of the nineteenth century, British Large Whites were already establishing themselves all over the world. Innovative pedigree breeders, such as Sanders Spencer of the Holywell herd near Huntingdon, were exporting breeding stock as far afield as Australia, Argentina, Canada and Russia, as well as most countries in Europe.

The Large White has proved itself as a rugged and hardy breed that can withstand variations in climate and other environmental factors. Their ability to cross with and improve other breeds has given them a leading role in commercial pig production systems and breeding pyramids around the world.

While the Large White was originally developed as an active and outdoor breed, they do very well in intensive production systems. They and their descendants, the Yorkshire, are to be found in practically all crossbreeding and rotational breeding programmes using two or more breeds. The sows of the breed

have an enviable reputation as dams, and form the foundation of the classic FI hybrid gilt. Modern breeding programmes have developed separate sire and dam lines to produce purebred Large White terminal sires that excel in growth rate and lean meat percentage and are incorporated in most terminal sire breeding programmes. They can definitely stamp uniformity and quality on a pen of pigs from almost any breed or type of dam.

In the early 1970s the development of modern performance testing programmes led to an increase in worldwide demand for Large White breeding stock from the United Kingdom. In the first three years of that decade more than 8,500 pedigree Large Whites were exported to all parts of the world. Then once again in the early 1990s, the switch in the USA from payment on liveweight to payment on lean meat percentage led to another great wave of exports of Large White genetics from Britain. The leading British breeders of today have followed in the footsteps of their Victorian predecessors with exports to over sixty countries around the world, justifying the Large White's undeniable claim to be the 'world's favourite breed'.

The Breed Standard of Excellence

Head: Moderately long, face slightly dished, snout broad and not too much turned up, light jowl, wide between the eyes and ears; neither jaw should be overshot.

Ears: Long and pricked, slightly forward and fringed with hair.

Neck: Clean, medium length, and proportionately full to the shoulders.

Shoulders: Medium to good width, displaying open shoulder blades when the head is down, free from coarseness and not too deep before maturity.

Back, loin and ribs: Long, with slightly arched back and wide from neck to rump. Ribs well sprung to allow good muscling; free from weakness behind shoulder and loin.

Hams: Broad, well muscled at the side and back, and deep to the hocks; ample length from pin bone to tail.

Tail: Well set and strong.

Underline: At least fourteen sound and well spaced teats free from supernumeraries; for boars, at least three on each side in front of the sheath.

Legs: Straight, set well apart; plenty of bone and adequate length.

Pasterns: Short, strong and springy.

Feet: Strong, with even cleys.

Action: Firm and free.

Skin: Fine, white, free from wrinkles and black and blue spots.

Coat: Silky and free from 'roses'.

THE POT-BELLIED PIG

Breed History

Originating in Vietnam, the Pot-Bellied pig is a breed of domestic pig that has been around for centuries. Smaller than the American or European pig that weighs in the region of 450kg (1,000lb), a Pot Belly can range in

Pot-Bellied pig.

weight from 27kg to 135kg (60lb to 300lb). The average weight of the Pot Belly is between 78kg and 90kg (150lb and 200lb).

These pigs are distinguishable not only by their small size, but also by their upright ears, straight tail, sway back and of course their rounded pot belly. It is believed that at one time these pigs were kept as household pets both in China and Vietnam, long before dogs became pets.

Pot-Bellied Pigs as Pets

During the 1990s, the Pot-Bellied pig was increasingly common as a household pet, their loving temperament and their ability to bond well with humans making them desirable. Highly intelligent, these pigs could also be easily trained.

Most people, however, had difficulty realizing that these animals took between three and five years to fully mature, and that full grown they would often not fit into their surroundings. This often resulted in full-grown Pot-Bellied pigs being abandoned in parks and other areas when they became too much for the owners to deal with.

In Vietnam and China the Pot-Bellied pig has become a food source rather than a pet, but with the introduction of larger swine for food consumption, the Pot-Bellied pig began to die out in China. Seeing the likelihood of this happening in Vietnam as well, the government there subsidizes farmers committed to continuing to raise these small pot-bellied swine.

Characteristics of the Pot-Bellied Pig

- Highly sensitive nature
- Sway back
- Long straight tail
- Small pointed ears
- Large belly that hangs very close to the ground
- Various colours
- Soft silky coat

GLOSSARY

afterbirth   The placenta and foetal membranes expelled from the uterus after birth.

amniotic sac   The fluid bag in which the piglet develops.

anaesthetic   Drug used to temporarily reduce or take away sensation, usually so that otherwise painful procedures or surgery can be performed.

anthelmintic   Drugs that expel parasitic worms from the body, by either stunning or killing them.

antibiotics   Drugs that inhibit the growth of, or destroy bacteria.

antresi ani   No anus.

bloodlines   The lines of descent in a pedigree.

boar   Sexually active male pig.

boar taint   The smell or flavour in meat from a male pig.

breed standard   The standards of excellence set by the breed societies for each pig.

cannibalism   Killing and eating or partially eating piglets.

castration   Removal of the testicles.

colostrum   First milk produced after birth.

condition score   To measure the fat and body condition of the pig.

crèche   Safe place for young piglets.

creep   Area that piglets can access but the sow cannot.

cull   To kill.

farrow   Give birth.

flushing   Feeding up well prior to mating.

gestation   Period of pregnancy.

gilt   Female pig that has not had piglets.

hernia   Protrusion of the intestine through the wall of the abdominal cavity.

hogging   Female pig showing signs that she is ready to mate with the boar.

infertile   In the female: unable to conceive a litter; in the male: unable to fertilize the female eggs.

inguinal ring   Opening through which the testicle passes when it descends into the scrotum.

intramuscular   Into the muscle.

litter Group of piglets all born from one mating.

metritis Inflammation of the womb.

oxytocin Hormone used to encourage contractions in the female pig.

pedigree Record of the provenance of an animal going back several generations.

quarantine Isolation for a period of time to prevent the spread of disease.

reabsorb The sow takes up or receives back into her system the foetuses and all matter relating to them.

rupture Tear.

scan X-ray by ultrasound.

scours Diarrhoea.

scenting Leaving a distinctive odour.

service Mating.

sites Places to inject.

sow Female pig that has had piglets.

stillborn Born dead or lifeless.

subcutaneous Under the skin.

ultrasound The application of ultrasonic waves for the imaging of internal structures.

uterus Womb.

vulva Vagina.

wallow (noun) Muddy, wet place where pigs can coat themselves with mud as a protection against the sun.

FURTHER INFORMATION

FURTHER READING

Charagu, Dr Patrick K. *Congenital Defects in Pigs: 1. Hernias and Ridglings* (2005).

Compassion in World Farming 'Tooth Clipping' www.ciwf.org.uk (2010).

European Commission's Scientific Veterinary Committee (SVC) *Report on Pig Welfare and Tail Docking* (1997).

Gill, Dr Pinder *Colostrum: Food For Life* (June 2002).

Hoeven, Eric van der *Colostrum: Let Them Drink!* (2006).

USEFUL ADDRESSES

British Pig Association (BPA)
British Pig Association
Trumpington Mews
40b High Street
Trumpington
Cambridge CB2 9LS
www.britishpigs.org

Berkshire Pig Breeders Club
Secretary: Mrs T Bretherton
Eastbourne, Moss House Lane
Westby with Plumpton
Kirkham PR4 3PE
Tel: 01772 673245
www.berkshirepigs.org
gracebank.pigs@yahoo.co.uk

British Saddleback Pig Breeders Club
Secretary: Mr Richard Lutwyche
Freepost (GL442)
Cirencester
Gloucestershire GL7 5BR
Tel: 01285 860229
www.saddlebacks.org.uk
mail@saddlebacks.org.uk

Gloucestershire Old Spot Pig Breeders Club
Secretary: Mr Richard Lutwyche
Freepost (GL442)
Cirencester
Gloucestershire GL7 5BR
Tel: 01285 860229
www.oldspots.com
info@oldspots.org.uk

Large Black Pig Breeders Club
Secretary: Mrs Janice Wood
20 Alice Street
Sale
Cheshire M33 3JF
Tel: 0161 976 4734
www.largeblackpigs.co.uk
kenworthyflock@fsmail.net

Middle White Pig Breeders Club
Secretary: Mrs Miranda Squire
Benson Lodg
50 Old Slade Lane
Iver
Buckinghamshire SL0 9DR
Tel: 01753 654166
www.middlewhite.co.uk
miranda@middlewhites.freeserve.co.uk

Oxford Sandy & Black Pig Society
Secretary: Mr Peter G. Colson
Field Farm, North Leigh
Witney
Oxon OX29 6TX
Tel: 01993 881207
Mob: 07850 185177
www.oxfordsandypigs.co.uk
info@fieldfarmoxford.co.uk

Tamworth Pig Breeders Club
Secretary: Mrs Lucy Hick
Hobland Cottage, East Ilsley
Newbury
West Berkshire RG20 7LE
Tel: 07747 034170
www.tamworthbreedersclub.co.uk
secretary@tamworthbreedersclub.co.uk

The Pedigree Welsh Pig Society
Office 12, Enterprise Centre
Bryn Road, Tondu
Bridgend, CF32 9BS
Tel: 01656 724 914
www.pedigreewelsh.com
info@pedigreewelsh.com

Wales and Border Counties Pig Breeders
Association
Secretary: Mrs Barbara Warren
www.pigsonline.org.uk

British Lop Pig Society
Secretary: Mr Frank Miller
Tel: 01948 880243
secretary@britishloppig.org.uk
www.britishloppig.org.uk

British Kunekune Pig Society
Hall Cottage, Radwinter Road
Sewards End, Saffron Walden
Essex CB10 2LR
www.britishkunekunesociety.org.uk

Compassion in World Farming
River Court, Mill Lane
Godalming
Surrey GU7 1EZ
Tel: 01483 521 953
www.ciwf.org.uk/

Rare Breeds Survival Trust (RBST)
Stoneleigh Park
Nr Kenilworth
Warwickshire CV8 2LG
General Enquiries: 024 7669 6551

Deerpark Pedigree Pigs (AI)
Robert Overen
Bellaghy
Magherafelt
Northern Ireland BT45 8LE
Tel: 028 79386287
028 79386558
Email: info@deerpark-pigs.com

Welfare of Animals in Transport (WIT)
Email: wit@animalhealth.gsi.gov.uk

Department of Food and Rural Affairs
(DEFRA)
www.defra.gov.uk

Farmrite (Farm Supplies)
Farmrite Animal Health Ltd
9 Cecil Street
Portadown
Co. Armagh
Northern Ireland
BT62 3AT
Tel: 028 3839 4900
www.farmrite.co.uk

Mole Valley Farmers (Farm Supplies)
For sow milk replacer – Volac Faramate
Email: info@molevalleyfarmers.com
www.molevalleyfarmers.com

Hyperdrug
For Collate Kickstart for piglets, Flubenol
individual wormer, veterinary supplies,
online pharmacy
Tel: 0844 7000801
www.hyperdrug.co.uk

Catac
For pet supplies, small teats, bottles etc.
Catac Products UK Ltd, 3–5 Chiltern Trading
Estate, Earl Howe Road, Holmer Green, High
Wycombe, Bucks, HP15 6QT
Tel: 08453 70 70 40
www.catac.co.uk

Supplies for Smallholders
Breeding record books, medicine record
books and other supplies
Bridge Farm, Fen Road, Donington, Spald-
ing, Lincolnshire, PE11 4X
Tel: 07981 336098
www.suppliesforsmallholders.co.uk

Country Smallholding magazine (available
from newsagents)
Country Smallholding, Archant Devon, Fair
Oak Close, Exeter Airport Business Park,
Clyst Honiton, Nr Exeter, EX5 2UL
Editor: Simon McEwan
Tel: 01392 888481
Fax: 01392 888499
Email: editorial.csh@archant.co.uk

Smallholder magazine (available from
newsagents)
Editor: Liz Wright
Hook House
Hook Road
Wimblington
March
Cambs, PE15 0QL
Tel: 01354 741538
Mob: 07967 339686
Fax: 01354 741182
Email: liz.wright1@btconnect.com

Practical Pigs magazine (available from
newsagents)
Kelsey Publishing Ltd
Cudham Tithe Barn
Berry's Hill
Cudham
Kent, TN16 3AG
Tel: 01959 541444
Fax: 01959 541400

Homefarmer magazine
Editors: Ruth Tott and Paul Melnyczuk
Tel: 01772 633444
www.homefarmer.co.uk

USEFUL WEBSITES AND FORUMS

www.thepigsite.com
www.rivercottage.net
www.accidentalsmallholder.net
www.downsizer.net

INDEX